Daring to Speak for God:
Sermons, Meditations, Devotions, and Lectures

Janeth Norfleete Day

Parson's Porch Books

Daring to Speak for God: Sermons, Meditations, Devotions, and Lectures
ISBN: Softcover 978-1-949888-56-0
Copyright © 2016 by Janeth Norfleete Day

All rights reserved. No part of this book may be reproduced or transmitted in any form or by any means, electronic or mechanical, including photocopying, recording, or by any information storage and retrieval system, without permission in writing from the publisher.

Permission to use extended quote by Frederick Buechner on pages 34-36, and quotes on pages 38 and 39 was granted by Frederick Buechner Library Assets, LLC, www.frederickbuechner.com.

To order additional copies of this book, contact:

Parson's Porch Books
1-423-475-7308
www.parsonsporch.com

Parson's Porch Books is an imprint of Parson's Porch & Company (PP&C) in Cleveland, Tennessee. PP&C is an innovative company which raises money by publishing books of noted authors, representing all genres. All donations from contributors and profits from publishing are shared with the poor.

Daring to Speak for God:

Sermons, Meditations, Devotions, and Lectures

Table of Contents

Preface	7
Introduction	11

Sermons

A Ministry of Love	17
Train Up a Child	26
Son, Servant, Savior	40
God's Reputation at Stake	53
If Possible, Thy Will Be Done	59
Who Dares to Speak About Jesus?	65
I Press On	72
The Sufficiency of Grace	81
Wade in the Water	88
A Close Encounter of the Divine Kind	94
One Necessary Thing	100
Resurrection Power	104

Meditations

Paraphrase on Proverbs 31	113
Spiritual Formation Charge	114
By My Spirit	118

Devotions

The Better Thing	123
Christian Hospitality	125
God's Faithfulness	127
Where Is Your God?	129

Lectures

Who Was the Samaritan Woman?	133
Jesus Loves the Children of the World?	145

Preface

For seventeen years, in one capacity or another, I was privileged to teach students preparing for ministry at Beeson Divinity School in Birmingham, Alabama. During those years, it was not uncommon for students to ask for copies of my dissertation research or a sermon I had preached. As a result of their requests, and following my retirement in 2009, I thought at some point I might pull together a collection such as this. Denise George, a gifted writer and teacher of aspiring writers, has encouraged me to publish these items numerous times. Her enthusiasm stimulated me to give positive thought to the idea of publishing my writings, but I have persistently allowed other pursuits to derail my efforts until now.

In the spring of 2015, I was asked to teach a four-week class on "Writing as a Spiritual Practice" for my church, Vestavia Hills Baptist Church in Birmingham, Alabama. The class drew more interest and participants than I anticipated, and to sustain that interest, our pastor, Gary Furr, initiated a monthly writers group for all who wanted to continue their writing activities. I have been a regular participant in that group, and the other members have provided me generous affirmations of my work.

In fall 2015, Gary Furr published a collection of some sermons, prayers, and songs he had written over the course of his ministry. He encouraged me to consider publishing a collection of my own work with the same company he dealt with, Parson's Porch & Company. Inspired by his success and his support, I began pulling together this collection of my writings and editing them for publication.

The individual pieces in this book have been long in the making, for the most part. The earliest sermon dates from 1992, and the latest piece was prepared in 2015. At the head of each individual item I have written a short statement about the occasion that called it forth, so here I explain only why this collection and why now.

In December 2015, when I began to see an end to this project, I contacted David Tullock at Parson's Porch, told him a bit about myself, mentioned Gary Furr's name, and asked if he would consider publishing this collection. His immediate and positive response was the catalyst I needed to set myself a deadline, and thus, finally, make this volume a reality. Thank you, David, for helping me turn my dream into a tangible result.

As with all authors, when it comes time to express gratitude to those whose support and help have made a work possible, I can't begin to name them all. However, in addition to Denise George and Gary Furr, whom I mentioned above, I want to thank Ann Knight and Sheryl Churchill Buckner, the other regular members of our "Write After Lunch" group, for their unfailing attentiveness to my writing and the useful suggestions they have made for improving it. Iva Jewel Tucker, a long-time friend and professional editor, kindly read this entire manuscript with her keen eye and made a number of suggestions for improvement. Naturally, I take responsibility for any errors of content or style that remain.

My brothers, Bud, Joe, and Jim, along with their families, have always supported and encouraged me in my various activities, and this writing project is no exception. The former students who continue to inspire and motivate me, the members of my church who unfailingly convey their approval of my work, and the dear friends who have patiently listened to my ideas and urged me to put fingers to keyboard, have all contributed to the writing of this book. Jill Sciacca is preeminent among them and generously offered suggestions for improving the wording.

My parents, Herschel H. and Louise Sanders Day, were committed believers who maintained a Christian home and nurtured their children with abundant love and faithful lives. They taught us, by word and example, that the only life worth living was one dedicated to God. I consider them one of God's finest gifts to me and am forever grateful for their godly lives and legacy.

My dearest friend, Barbara Kimbrel, orders my life and tends to many tasks so as to free up my time for writing. Her desire to see this book become a reality has provided a steady diet of support and encouragement.

Without Dean Timothy George's expectations and preaching assignments, I might never have undertaken such a daunting task as "daring to speak for God." His affirmations of my work, across the years, and his friendship continue to enrich my life and ministry.

And finally, no study and explication of the Bible has much value unless God's Holy Spirit inspires and attends it. I cannot begin to express my gratitude to God for the joy and opportunity of sharing some of what God has revealed to me in the course of my teaching and preaching.

Soli deo gloria

Introduction

My calling from God, as I understood it, was not to preach, but to teach. Some would declare there isn't much difference, and in my case, that is likely true. Those who analyze sermons would probably describe my sermons as teaching messages but I think that is acceptable. I have come to believe that whether a person's Christian vocation is to preach or to teach, both activities, at their root, are calls to make known the message of God as revealed in Scripture. While I have never sought the opportunity to proclaim the Word of God in sermonic form, some occasions have sought me, and the sermons included here are the result.

I prepared my very first sermon as a requirement of my seminary curriculum. It required every student to take a course in preaching, and as the culmination of that study to write a sermon. I do not recall much about that particular sermon, but as I neared graduation, the Dean of the Divinity School invited me to preach in the seminary chapel service. Even now I remember the swell of pride at his confidence in me, implicit in the invitation, followed by the staggering realization of the responsibility inherent in the assignment.

As I prepared, however, excitement came—excitement from the conviction I felt of being led by the Holy Spirit. Recognizing my own sense of inadequacy, I prayed earnestly for guidance and insight as I chose a text and poured over it. During that process I began to sense a power at work beyond myself—the inspiration of God's Holy Spirit. The Spirit's power generated in me a growing sense of elation at the opportunity to share what God was teaching me. When the time came to preach that sermon, I felt it as a fountain welling up in me that must overflow.

That same process has characterized every sermon I have prepared since then. Several years later, when I had been recruited back to Beeson Divinity School as a member of the faculty, I had other opportunities to preach. Dean Timothy George firmly believed the students should, from time to time, hear sermons preached by their professors. Consequently, across the years he gave me several preaching assignments for our weekly chapel services. Sometimes the text or topic was assigned, sometimes I was free to choose my own.

Over time, other opportunities presented themselves. One of my former students invited me, three years in a row, to lead a weekend Bible study at his church, which included preaching during the Sunday morning worship service. On occasion, my own pastor, Gary Furr, at Vestavia Hills Baptist Church, asked me to fill the pulpit for him on a Sunday morning. In every case, I found saturation in the biblical text, coupled with earnest prayer for discernment and direction, kindled the familiar stirring in my heart and spirit with a message that pleaded to be proclaimed.

I prepared the meditations and devotions by a similar process and for a variety of settings. Most of the meditations I composed for the midweek communion service at my church. The devotions I wrote in the style of a daily guide such as *Open Windows* or *The Upper Room*, during a writing class I took with Denise George. I have not previously published them.

The two lectures address topics to which I devoted significant time and research. The one on racial reconciliation I developed during a sabbatical the fall semester of 2005. Dean George often reminded the faculty at Beeson Divinity School that we had a "stewardship of geography" by virtue of our location in Birmingham, Alabama. We regularly offered a course in Racial Reconciliation that included lectures by many of our faculty members and community leaders. During my sabbatical at the Institute for Ecumenical and Cultural Research at St. John's University in Collegeville, Minnesota, I had plans of collecting those lectures into a book, which would include my own contribution among them. Other projects and demands on my time caused me to lose that opportunity, but I include here the lecture I prepared and delivered at the Institute based on my research there.

The second lecture is based on my doctoral dissertation on the Samaritan woman whom Jesus encountered in Chapter 4 of John's Gospel. My dissertation explored how that character has been interpreted throughout history by the Church, in literature, and in art. My unique contribution was to examine the Samaritan woman through the lens of literary and social-scientific criticism, which led me to an interpretation of her character different from the one most often put forward by New Testament scholars. I proposed that she might have been a pious victim of her culture whom Jesus sought intentionally rather than the immoral person others thought her to be. As I have shared my interpretation in a variety of venues, many have asked how they might obtain it in written form. I include the lecture here in response to their requests.

Charles Colson, the well-known founder of Prison Fellowship, wrote a book in 1985, titled *Who Speaks for God?* That title caught my attention and led me to reflect on what a daring endeavor it is to be a spokesperson for the Almighty. Each time I have preached a sermon, my soul prayer has been that the words I spoke might be worthy of the God they sought to honor. Thus, the title of this book: *Daring to Speak for God*. I offer here sermons, meditations, devotions, and the two lectures that I have composed over some twenty years. I have made minor revisions to facilitate reading them instead of hearing them. I pray they have the power to enrich you in reading them as they blessed me in their preparation and delivery.

J. Norfleete Day

Sermons

During my fourth year in divinity school, Dean George invited me to speak in the weekly chapel service. It was a daunting assignment to preach my first sermon before my professors and classmates, but this is the message I felt led to preach.

A Ministry of Love
1 John 4:8-21; John 13:34-35
Beeson Divinity School
April 28, 1992

"They'll know we are Christians by our love. . . .. They'll know we are Christians by our love." Most of us know that line from the familiar song and recognize it as Jesus' words to his disciples recorded for us in John 13. On that final night before Jesus' crucifixion, in those last precious hours he spent with his disciples, he said to them, "A new command I give to you, that you love one another. As I have loved you, so you must love one another. By this, all will know that you are my disciples, if you have love one for another."

It is interesting that Jesus called this a new command because, in fact, the command to love was not new at all. In Leviticus, Moses had passed on to the Hebrew People God's command that they love their neighbor, so the command to love was not new at all. What was new was the instruction Jesus gave about how they were to love.

In Leviticus the command is to love your neighbor as yourself. Jesus said, "Love one another as I have loved you." What was it that was so distinct and so special about Jesus' kind of love that he felt confident to assure his disciples if they would love one another in that same manner, everyone would recognize there was something unique and different about their love from everything else that passed for love in the world?

I think we find the answer to that in Matthew 5:43-48. This, of course, is part of Jesus' Sermon on the Mount, and in this particular portion Jesus had begun by assuring the people he had not come to destroy the law, but rather to fulfill it. Then, he began to discuss various precepts of the law in an attempt to expand and enhance their understanding so they would grasp the motivation and spirit and attitude behind those legal requirements they had become so fixated upon.

Jesus said in verse 43: "You have heard it was said, 'Love your neighbor and hate your enemy.' But I tell you, 'Love your enemies, and pray for those who persecute you that you may be children of your Father in heaven. He causes his sun to rise on the evil and the good and sends rain on the righteous and the unrighteous. If you love those who love you, what reward will you get? Are not even the tax collectors doing that? And if you greet only your brothers, what are you doing more than others? Do not even pagans do that? Be perfect, therefore, as your heavenly Father is perfect."

Jesus began by stating the love command in the way the Jews had come to interpret it and in the manner by which they practiced it. But, it is important to note that nowhere in Scripture is the command given to hate one's enemies. Rather, this seems to have been a man-made rationalization that had developed through the years and become part of the interpretation and practice of this rule as the Jews lived it out in daily life.

The Jewish conception of a neighbor was very narrowly defined. To a Jew, his neighbor was a fellow Jew. A Pharisee would restrict it even to a fellow Pharisee. So the Jewish people had very narrowly circumscribed the application of this command in their lives. And Jesus had not yet expanded their understanding of who their neighbor was by sharing that famous parable about the Good Samaritan.

So Jesus says to them, "Love of neighbor is good, but it isn't nearly enough. The divine ideal is not simply that you love those who are like you, those with whom you feel comfortable, who are sympathetic with you, those with whom you share a common racial, religious and cultural heritage. The divine ideal, God's intent is that you should love everyone, even those who are your enemies."

Jesus wasn't just adding another category. He wasn't just saying love your neighbors and your enemies. He was using these two categories in a merism, giving the two extremes of neighbor and enemy, and thereby including everyone in between. He was including those people, that vast multitude of individuals, whom we encounter every day as we go about our business, for whom we have no particular like or dislike, but who share life on this earth with us.

I am haunted by the face of a woman I met on the streets of downtown Birmingham. I encountered her the first time one day on my lunch hour. A group of my colleagues and I were walking downtown to eat, and this woman approached us on the sidewalk. She said, "Can you help me?" We stopped and asked what she needed, and she said she just needed a little money to tide her over, that she was new in town and looking for work. She was short of funds, and could we spare a few dollars?

It was immediately obvious to all of us that her prospects of getting a job were very slim. Her hair was matted and straggly, her clothing was worn and ill fitting, and several of her teeth were missing. She was the classic case of a beggar, and yet there was something appealing about her, something that compelled my interest. We all gave her money, but walked away feeling very dissatisfied. We recognized we had only scratched the surface of her need, yet we didn't know how to go about meeting her greater needs.

She became a fixture on the streets of downtown Birmingham. It became impossible to walk down the street at lunchtime without encountering her. I even got in the habit of slipping a dollar into my pocket before I left my office because I knew I would see her and she would ask that inevitable question, "Can you help me?"

But she troubled me. I went away after every encounter with her feeling there was so much more I should be doing, but not knowing how. One day when she approached me with the usual question, "Can you help me?" I said, "Do you have a place to stay?"

Completely ignoring my question, she repeated, "Can you help me?"

I said, "Do you have a place to stay?"

The third time she said, "Can you help me?"

And I repeated, "Do you have a place to stay?"

She became very nervous and said, "The old people I stay with asked me not to say where I live, and I don't want to make trouble for nobody. I just don't want to cause any trouble." I immediately assured her I didn't want to cause trouble either. I was just concerned to know if she had a place to stay. But her remarks confirmed what I had already surmised: someone was using her as a professional panhandler.

I agonized about this woman. I dreamed about her. I prayed about her but the answer didn't come. Until one day I was reading in Malcolm Muggeridge's wonderful little book about Mother Teresa, *Something Beautiful for God*. In that book he quotes Mother Teresa saying something about her work among the indigents in Calcutta. She said, "The thing these people need most, more than food, and clothing and shelter—although they desperately need those—is to be wanted. Their status as outcasts, which is imposed on them by their poverty, is the most agonizing thing of all."

That statement spoke to my heart in a very moving way and immediately I thought of "my" woman on the street. And I determined that is what I wanted to do for her—I wanted to make her feel wanted. So, I decided the next time I encountered her I would spend some time with her. Maybe we would just walk along the street. Maybe we would sit down and talk together. One way or another, I was going to be present with her.

Most people meeting her on the street would look away, pretending they didn't see her, because they knew the familiar question was coming: "Can you help me?" I decided the reason she always approached me was because at least I looked at her, which most people didn't.

The next day I could hardly wait for my lunch hour to come. I declined all invitations and set out by myself so I would be sure to have time to spend with her. I went at the usual time and followed my usual route, but I saw no sign of her. I was deeply disappointed, but resolved to try again the next day. Maybe our paths had just not crossed that day for some reason. The second day the same thing happened. I went at the usual time and followed my usual route—no sign of her.

The unfortunate ending of this story is that I have never seen that woman again, at least not in person. But I see her almost daily in my mind's eye because she is a vivid reminder to me of my failure. I had an opportunity—a unique and special opportunity—to love her as Jesus has loved me—and I failed. But I am convinced she is exactly the kind of person Jesus was including here in this command for us to love everyone we encounter.

Allow me to paraphrase what Jesus said: You claim to be Christians, and as such, you are called by my name, called to model the love of your Father in heaven. You're called his children, and you should be showing and demonstrating his character in your daily lives. So think about God. Think about how God loves.

When God brings the sun out every morning, he doesn't cause it to shine just on the people who do good things and not on the people who do bad things. When God sends the rain, it doesn't fall only on the just people and not on the unjust. God loves every person he has created, and he bestows his blessings universally. If you want to be called children of God, his sons and daughters, that is how you should love.

Think about how it is with people who are not Christians. If you love only those who love you, Jesus says, how are you different from the rest of the world? How are you different from those people whom you consider least worthy—those hated tax collectors, whom you regard as traitors because they work for the Roman government and extract exorbitant taxes from their own people? They are always ceremonially unclean because of their regular contact with Gentiles, and you think they are among the lowest form of life there is, and yet, even they love those who love them. It may only be their wives and their mothers, but they do love the people who love them.

Consider the simple matter of offering a greeting, that simple means by which we acknowledge an individual's personhood. A greeting is the means by which we show respect for a person's dignity and worth as one of God's creations. If you only speak to the people who speak to you, how are you any different than the pagan people you think are so bad?

Have you ever been to a church supper on Wednesday night and seen the people who gather every week at the same table and save seats for their friends so they can sit together? They don't give a thought to people who may not have a little group with whom to sit, or the newcomer who may be in their midst. It's so common to human nature, and yet Jesus said, "That isn't the way at all. You are called to be different. Your love is supposed to be like the love of your Father."

A certain minister in the northeast told of receiving a phone call one day in 1988 from the International Olympic Committee. He was asked if he would consider serving as chaplain for the Olympic Games to be held that year in Korea. He couldn't begin to describe the excitement and joy he felt over receiving that offer. He immediately and eagerly agreed to serve.

In the ensuing months, he anticipated with great joy the privilege of this once-in-a-lifetime opportunity that was going to be his. He enthusiastically shared the news with friends far and near. When the time came, he went to the Games, and he served, experiencing firsthand, although vicariously, "the thrill of victory and the agony of defeat." He had the opportunity to meet and get to know world-class athletes, people who had devoted years of their lives to developing their bodies, perfecting their sports skills so that somehow in this competition they could beat out the other competitors and be recognized and acclaimed and honored as the best in their sport.

It was, indeed, everything he had hoped the experience would be, and when he returned home, he basked in the afterglow for weeks. He never tired of recounting to family and friends the wonder and joy of his experience.

Several months later, the same minister received another phone call, this time from the organizers of the Special Olympics, those games held for handicapped children who will never have the opportunity to participate in the regular Olympic competitions. He was asked, since he had served as chaplain for the regular Olympics, if he would serve in the same role for the Special Olympics.

He felt nothing of the same joy and excitement from this invitation that he had experienced with the first phone call, but he did feel a sense of responsibility, so he agreed to serve. When the time came, he went to the Games, he did serve as chaplain, and all went as expected until the final day of the competitions.

Time came for the 100-yard dash, and seven young children took their places at the starting line. When the starting gun fired, those seven little bodies lunged forward, awkwardly, clumsily, each in some way limited by his or her impairment. Each was trying valiantly to stay inside his or her lane on the track.

About halfway around the track, one of the little girls stumbled and fell. As she fell, she cried out—a loud, agonizing, desperate cry that was heard throughout the stands. Immediately, silence fell. In that moment, reacting to her cry, the other six children stopped. One by one, they looked back toward the sound of that cry and saw the girl who had fallen.

Almost as if in slow motion, those six children turned around and ran back to the girl who had fallen. They gathered around her on the ground, spoke comforting words, and dried her tears. They helped her to her feet, and arm in arm, those seven children finished the race together.

The minister said in that moment he was struck powerfully by the truth of the Gospel. He said, "I had been so thrilled and excited by the regular Olympic Games, by seeing the performances of athletes who strove to beat out the other runners so they could earn honor and acclaim for themselves. But here, I had just seen a classic demonstration of the kind of love Jesus came to teach and model for us.

"This race of the handicapped children is like the race we run in life because at some time each one of us is like the child fallen on the track. We need a helping hand, comforting words, and caring people to help us get back in the race, so we all can finish together."

He said as he looked around in the stands through the tears in his own eyes, he saw tears on the faces of all the people around him. They, too, had been touched and moved by witnessing the unexpected caring and compassion of the children on the track. Those children had shown they cared more about one another than they cared about winning any trophies or honors.

Jesus said when we love others in the way he loved us, then our love will be like the love of the Father—perfect, mature, complete. We will model him as true daughters and sons of our heavenly Father.

"They'll know we are Christians by our love." Who knows that you are a Christian by your love?

When I returned to Beeson Divinity School as a faculty member, I learned that the focus for that year's chapel services was personal testimonies of the faculty. Consequently, in spring 1997, I preached the following message.

Train Up a Child
Proverbs 22:6
Beeson Divinity School
March 17, 1997

I have no memory of life without God. I was fortunate to be born into a Christian home to devout parents. When I think about my earliest memories, the names God and Jesus are as much a part of my memory as Mother and Daddy. We had a custom in our home: every evening before we went to bed we would gather as a family in the living room for Scripture reading and prayer. Before we children were able to read, Mother and Dad would read the Bible, and then we would all kneel in front of the sofa, join hands, and each of us would voice our prayer.

As little tykes our prayers would be "Now I lay me down to sleep," but in time we learned to pray with our own words. When we had said our prayers, then Mother and Dad would pray, calling each child's name and offering a particular prayer on our behalf.

As we children grew older and learned to read, we were allowed to take a turn reading the Scripture aloud for the family. Those devotional times had a profound effect on me. Even years later after I left home, the memory of those family prayer times and knowing that my parents and brothers were praying for me every night by name, gave me comfort and courage in many lonely and trying moments.

When I was six years old, I asked Jesus to come into my heart at the prompting of my older brother who was eight at the time. I don't remember a lot of the details other than he and I sitting on the bed in my room, talking together after attending a revival service. At some point in the conversation, my brother asked, "Why don't you ask Jesus to come into your heart?"

I don't recall whether I spoke aloud my response to him or if I only spoke in my heart to God, but I said, "I want to." That was for me the first formal declaration of my relationship with God.

I remember my first prayer, apart from those family nighttime devotions and blessings for the food at meal times, when I was seven years old. We had moved to Moultrie, Georgia, and I had begun attending a new school. One afternoon, by prearrangement, I went with a group of girls to a Brownie Scout meeting. One of the mothers drove us to the meeting at the Scout building, and my parents were to pick me up afterward.

I suppose the meeting got over earlier than expected, and most of the other girls left with their parents. I thought I remembered how we had gotten there, so I decided to walk back to the school. It didn't take long before I realized I didn't remember any of the things I was seeing and I was hopelessly lost. The only thing I knew to do was to pray, which I did. When I opened my eyes and lifted my head after praying, I saw just ahead of me a man and his wife sitting on their porch.

I walked to the gate at the front of their yard and asked if they could give me directions to the school. They said, "Which school?" Oops! That was a problem because I didn't know there was more than one. With a series of questions, they managed to get enough of a description from me to figure out where I needed to be. I had wandered far enough that it required getting into their car and letting them drive me there.

When I think about it now I'm surprised that they left me there alone. I went and sat down on the front steps of the school to wait for Mother and Dad to appear. It was one of those schools built of red brick with wide steps leading up to its imposing double front doors and huge white columns holding up the roof over the entry way.

I sat down beside one of those columns and eagerly watched the street for our car. Time, as you know, seems endless when you are waiting, so before long I was feeling discouraged. I was also starting to feel a little scared, so I developed a routine. I put my arms around my knees, buried my face in my lap, and prayed desperately for Mother and Dad to come. After praying for what seemed like long minutes, which were probably only seconds, I would look up hoping to see my parents come to the rescue.

It only took about five or six sequences of doing that before God did answer my prayer. My parents did drive up. I'm not sure who was more relieved, they or I. They had been driving frantically through all the neighborhoods between the school and the Scout building looking for me. Years later in reminiscing about that event, my mother said the most forlorn picture she could remember was seeing that tiny little girl sitting there beside those huge columns.

I learned something valuable about God out of that experience. I learned that God really was with me, wherever I was, that God would hear my prayers, and God would answer my prayers. That's an important thing for a seven-year-old to know.

During my childhood and adolescence, I was active in all the usual Baptist church activities—Sunday School, worship, Training Union, Girls' Auxiliary, Vacation Bible School, and youth choir. When I graduated from high school, I made plans to go to college. I thought I wanted to go to Tulane. Now I have no idea why, but that was my goal at the time. However, the Lord had other plans, and I ended up at Howard College (now Samford University) in Birmingham, Alabama. Those were rich and rewarding years for me. I was active in a local church, the Baptist Student Union, and campus missions organizations.

When I graduated from Samford University, I floundered a bit trying to figure out what to do with myself. I had a fresh, crisp BA degree, but didn't know how I wanted to use it. I tried several things. I went to graduate school for a year in English, worked as a technical writer, did some substitute teaching, served two years in the Navy as a Personnel Officer, went back to school for a year to study pre-med, and finally came to grips with reality.

I realized that my gifts and abilities lay in the humanities rather than the sciences, so I enrolled in Library School at The University of Alabama in Tuscaloosa. When I received my master's degree in Library and Information Science, I thought I wanted to leave Alabama, so I went on an interviewing trip to Virginia and Tennessee. That was not as promising a trip as I had hoped it would be, and when I got back to Birmingham I had a message waiting for me from the Dean of the Library School.

He said Birmingham Public Library was looking for a Catalog Librarian and gave me contact information, in case I was interested. I went for an interview and was hired on the spot. At the time, given that my venture into Virginia and Tennessee hadn't gone very well and this job had practically fallen into my lap, I saw the Lord's hand in keeping me in Birmingham and putting me there. That sense was confirmed when, less than two years later, I was promoted from Junior Catalog Librarian to Associate Director for Technical Services, second only to the Director of the Library System.

Esther 4:14 became my habitual verse to describe that experience: "Who knows but that the Lord has brought you to the kingdom for such a time as this?" I knew that only through the Lord's leading was I there at all and in a position to receive such a fantastic promotion. It really was a case of being in the right place at the right time.

This was the era when libraries were just beginning to automate, to convert their card catalog files into digital format. There were two senior catalog librarians, but they were both long out of library school and library automation was foreign to them. I was a fresh, new library school graduate with one whole three-hour course in library automation. That was a valuable credential in those days, so I was chosen to oversee the conversion of the library's card catalog information into machine-readable form.

It was a challenging but very fulfilling experience for me working at the library. I developed professionally, had to grow into my role very quickly, taking on some major responsibilities. In time, I was also able to be involved in a major way in the design and construction of a new library building and renovation of the old library building. It was a fast-track journey from entry-level librarian to overseeing exciting new developments in library buildings and services.

Equally important at that time, God led me into a wonderful church situation where I experienced some giant strides of growth in my spiritual life. I found myself at South Avondale Baptist Church under the guidance and mentorship of the pastor, Dr. Buddy McGohon. Through his preaching and teaching, I began to think intentionally and seriously about my calling to serve God even though I was not in a church-related vocation.

At various times in my life, I had tried to convince the Lord that he should call me into foreign missions. God is hard to convince when he is not in agreement with what you want. I chased him for a number of years with that in mind, but it didn't happen. I had resigned myself to being a sort of "second-class" citizen in the kingdom and, therefore, free to pursue my secular profession.

But under Buddy McGohon's leadership, as I began to study the Bible and pray in a fresh and vibrant way, I began to understand that I actually had a ministry in my position at the library. God had placed me there for a reason. As I thought about my work there in terms of vocation, not just a career, I realized that I did have a real opportunity. Most people spend more of their waking hours on their job than they do anywhere else, so what happens on the job colors their whole life. It impacts how they relate to their families, and it impacts how they feel about themselves and how they feel about the world.

I made it my mission to make the library a place where people could enjoy coming to work, a place where Christian values were upheld, where Christian virtues were practiced, and where people were treated with respect and understanding. And even though I enjoyed my work and found fulfillment in it prior to that time, suddenly seeing it as a ministry and mission gave it a whole new meaning.

I remember one Sunday as I was leaving church, after having greeted Buddy, he said, "I came down to the library last week and I looked for you, but you weren't in your office." I said, "I'm sorry I missed you." And chuckling, he said, "I told the ladies at the Circulation Desk I was your pastor, and they seemed surprised to know that you had one." He'd said it jokingly, but often there's a kernel of truth in such comments.

As I thought about that conversation, I wanted Buddy to think well of me. I thought a lot of him, but I realized that in my zeal to maintain the separation of church and state, perhaps I had kept them too separate. It was important to me to be an example to my staff. I had a hundred and thirty-five people whom I could influence, who were looking to me for leadership. I wanted them to know that what was guiding me and the principles by which I was operating were Christian principles. I wanted them to catch hold of those values and share them. So that became a very purposeful and meaningful time in my life.

After a number of years, I reached one of those stages in life where you start to assess yourself and evaluate your circumstances. As I engaged in some self-examination, I realized that I had it made. My life was very comfortable. I was in a position of some prestige and influence; my peers respected me. I had been doing that job long enough that I felt I could handle whatever it might throw at me. My boss had total confidence in me and had rewarded me with generous raises and extensive benefits. To me it felt like being on "Easy Street."

Just about the time I began to coast, the Lord planted a nagging little question in my mind: "Do you suppose that God has done all these things for you and brought you to this place in your life just so you can sit here and enjoy them for the rest of your life?" I was not able to answer that question with a resounding "Yes!" but I wasn't ready to answer it with an overwhelming "No!" either.

But the question wouldn't go away; it kept nagging me. So, eventually I began to pray that if God had something else in mind for me, he would reveal it to me and make me willing to accept that revelation. I prayed that prayer over a period of two years. As time went by I even began to pray, "Lord, if you want me to leave here, stir up in me a growing discontent with being in this situation because I am really comfortable. I am really happy, so if I'm supposed to leave all this behind, make me dissatisfied with it."

And he did. Over that two-year period, God helped me realize he'd used me there just about as long as he intended to use me there. When I thought about my future, I realized that if I stayed there I would essentially be doing the same things I had been doing over the past years. The new things were mostly done and what lay before me was essentially managing and tweaking them.

That future didn't feel very satisfying. I realized I had a limited resource of energy and creativity that would be used in ways I wasn't sure were the best. Not that the work I was doing was a bad thing, but it can be far too easy to settle for the good instead of pursuing the best.

After two years of living with these questions, in May 1988, God gave me his answer. I was riding up the highway, on my way to Wake Forest, North Carolina, to attend the seminary graduation of my best friend. As we rode along, I was reading something related to the upcoming Sunday School lesson, and I paused to reflect on some new insight I had gained. In that pause, a dialogue began in my head that I'm convinced was divinely orchestrated. It went something like this:

First Voice: "I really do enjoy studying and teaching the Bible. I wish I had more time to do that. Wouldn't it be great if somebody would pay you to study and teach the Bible?"

Response: "They would if you taught in a seminary or university."

First voice: "Yes, but you need a seminary degree and a Ph.D. to do that."

Response: "Samford has just announced the establishment of a Divinity School. You could stay right here in Birmingham and get your seminary training. After that, if you still feel this is where the Lord is leading, you could go on and get your Ph.D."

That conversation took place in a rapid-fire series of thoughts, almost like a slide show. I knew immediately this was God's answer to my brooding question. If I were to sum up my response in one word, it would be "Eureka!" I had found it.

In spite of the euphoria and excitement I was feeling, I stuffed it because we were on our way to my friend's graduation. This was her big moment, not mine. But I did begin to think about what this revelation meant in practical terms. I realized it would take about ten years just to complete this necessary educational preparation. That challenging other voice responded with this question: "Where will you be in ten years if you don't do it?"

When we got to the seminary, in my friend's mailbox was a small book, a gift from one of the graduates to all members of the class. It was a collection of seminary commencement addresses. Glancing through the book that evening, an address by Frederick Buechner, delivered at Union Theological Seminary in Richmond, Virginia caught my attention. These words from his speech came to me as a direct word from God:

I am here . . . to be, however inadequately, a servant of Christ. . ... We are all here because of him. . ...

Our business is to be the hands and feet and mouths of One who has no other hands or feet or mouth except our own. It gives you pause. Our business is to work for Christ as surely as men and women in other trades work for presidents of banks or managers of stores or principals of high schools. Whatever salaries you draw, whatever fringe benefits you receive, your recompense will be ultimately from Christ. And a strange and unforeseeable and wondrous recompense I suspect it will be. And with many a string attached to it, too. Whatever real success you have will be measured finally in terms of how well you please not anyone else in this world . . . but only Christ, and I suspect the successes that please him best are very often the ones that we don't even notice. Christ is the one who will be hurt, finally, by your failures. If you are to be healed, comforted, sustained during the dark times that will come to you, as surely as they have come to everyone else who has gone into this strange trade, Christ will be the one to sustain you because there's no one else in all this world with love enough and power enough to do so. It is worth thinking about.

He [Christ] is our pilot, our guide, our true, fast, final friend and judge, but often when we need him most, he seems farthest away because he has always gone on ahead, leaving only the faint print of his feet on the path to follow. And the world blows leaves across the path. And branches fall. And darkness falls. We are, all of us, Mary Magdalene, who reached out to him at the end only to embrace the empty air. We are the ones who stopped for a bite to eat that evening at Emmaus, and, as soon as they saw who it was that was sitting there at the table with them, found him vanished from their sight. Abraham, Moses, Gideon, Rahab and Sarah, are all our brothers and sisters because, like them, we all must live *in faith*.[1]

I read that many times over the next few days. When I returned to Birmingham, I contacted Dr. George and began the process of making application to Beeson Divinity School. My plan was to continue working full time for two years while taking courses part time. At the end of those two years, I would reverse the arrangement--go to school fulltime and work part time. During that first two years I would get my affairs in order, my financial arrangements made, so I could support myself during the full-time school years.

Those two years brought numerous evidences and affirmations of God's blessing in what I was doing. My journal is full of them. At the end of two years, I made the planned change, and eagerly embraced the new arrangement of putting school first. As you would expect, I was very busy. I studied hard, and worked two part-time jobs, which left very little free time to spend with family and friends.

During that semester, my dad became quite ill. In talking with my mother I realized she was concerned Dad might not live through the winter. Her concern caused me concern, and I began to pray that if God would keep my parents alive through that semester and enable me to finish my coursework, I would make a change to my schedule in the spring semester. I would reduce my coursework load so I could spend intentional and regular time with my parents.

God honored that prayer. My parents lived through the fall semester, I completed my work, and in the spring I took a reduced load and began spending regular time with my mother and dad. I saw them often on weekends, and we

---

[1] Frederick Buechner, "The Road Goes On," in *A Room Called Remember* (San Francisco: Harper & Row, 1984), 140-141.

frequently shared meals together during the week—cherished and valuable time because I realized the importance of it.

On April 27 of that spring, my mother died suddenly and unexpectedly of a heart attack. It was a devastating loss, but I was so grateful God had forewarned me. I had precious memories of special time spent with her instead of guilt and regret for having missed the opportunities.

That decision to reduce my coursework also benefitted me in another way. It required me to extend my time at Beeson a year beyond what I had planned. In August, as that final year of study drew near, the Associate Dean called me. He said he had realized the need for a second class of introductory Greek that year, and asked if I would be interested in teaching it. Wasn't that what I was preparing to do? I saw God's provision and blessing written all over that development. I gladly accepted and was able to teach Greek during my final year as a student.

That experience confirmed for me that teaching would indeed be as fulfilling as I had imagined it would be. Apparently, it also convinced the Dean and faculty that I could do it successfully. The summer after I graduated, as I was preparing to go to Baylor University in Waco, Texas for my doctoral study, Dean George took me to lunch and invited me to come back to Beeson during the summers to teach in summer school. Once again, God's provision.

I came back and taught a class the summer after my first year at Baylor. Once again, Dean George took me to lunch and asked if I would like to teach again the next summer. Most definitely, I would. After I taught the second summer, Dean George took me to lunch and said, "I understand you'll be finishing your coursework at Baylor this coming year. How would you like to come back next fall and teach full time for us while you write your dissertation?"

Only if God has given you a vision and a dream and you have experienced his faithfulness over seven years in bringing that dream to fulfillment do you have some idea of what I felt in that moment. It was the culminating point of that whole experience and in that journey with God. And here I am.

But that isn't the end of the story, you know, because my story, like your story, isn't really about me. It's about God. It's about what God can do and will do with just an ordinary person who will be faithful.

Let me close with another sharing from Buechner's commencement address. He quotes a song that J.R.R. Tolkien has Bilbo Baggins sing in his book, *The Lord of the Rings*, which goes like this:

The Road goes ever on and on
Down from the door where it began
Now far ahead the Road has gone
And I must follow, if I can.
Pursuing it with eager feet
Until it joins some larger way
Where many paths and errands meet.
And whither then? I cannot say.

"I am the way," Jesus said. "I am the road." And in some foolish fashion, we are all on the road that is his, or such at least, is our hope and prayer. That is why we're here. There is not a shoe in this place that does not contain a foot of clay, a foot that drags, a foot that stumbles. But on just such feet we all seek to follow that road through a world where there are many other roads to follow, and hardly a one of them that is not more known, more assured, and more realizable.

But we have picked this road, or been picked by it.[2]

And whither then? Whither now? "I cannot say," the singer says, nor yet can I, but far ahead the road goes on, and we must follow, if we can, because it is our road, it is his road. It is the only road that matters when you come right down to it.

The world is full of dark shadows to be sure, the world without and the world within. And the road we've set off on is long, and hard, and often hard to find, but the word is trust. Trust the deepest intuitions of your own heart, trust the source of your greatest happiness, trust the road, and above all, trust him, trust God.[3]

---

[2] Ibid., 143-144.
[3] Ibid., 147-148.

I prepared this sermon for delivery at a Beeson Divinity School chapel service during the 2001-2002 school year when our Dean chose to focus on The Apostles' Creed. He assigned a phrase of the Creed to each chapel speaker and my assignment was "suffered under Pontius Pilate, was crucified, dead and buried."

Son, Servant, Savior
Beeson Divinity School
Isaiah 52:13—53:12
November 6, 2001

"Man of Sorrows! What a name for the Son of God . . ."
—P. P. Bliss

The affirmations of the Apostles' Creed that we have been considering have not prepared us for the statement we encounter today— *"suffered under Pontius Pilate, was crucified, dead and buried;"*

How unimaginable that suffering and death could come to God's Son!

Let me review the creedal statements that have gone before:

"I believe in God, the Father Almighty, Maker of Heaven and Earth."

This God is Almighty—He can do anything; he has all power, all might; He's the One who made the entire universe and all that inhabits it.

"I believe . . . in his only Son, Jesus Christ, our Lord,"

This is the unique and only son of the Almighty God, who made all things. And he is legitimately "Lord," if only by reason of his membership in the Trinity. It is natural to give God's only Son honor and position.

"Conceived by the Holy Spirit,"

It is a bit surprising to think of Jesus being "conceived," as we associate conception with a human biological process, but clearly He is still uniquely distinguished from human beings in that Jesus' conception is by supernatural means, through the Holy Spirit.

"Born of the Virgin Mary" is also surprising because we don't expect a member of the Trinity to be "born,"—another human biological process.

But there is still a remarkable difference from human beings in that his birth is "of a Virgin"—that's certainly something unknown to our human experience.

But this next line is totally incomprehensible—*"SUFFERED" under Pontius Pilate!*

Suffering is something we humans certainly understand, but divinity isn't supposed to suffer! Many people don't even think royalty, those human beings who have been elevated above their peers to special position, ought to suffer.

Do you remember the fairy tale about "The Princess and the Pea"?

There was a prince who wanted to marry a princess, but found that many who claimed to be princesses weren't real. So one night in the middle of a storm, a young woman who claimed to be a princess showed up at the city gate, soaked and frazzled. The prince's mother's scheme to determine if the princess was "real" was to put a pea on the bottom of her bed under 20 mattresses and another 20 eider-down comforters. The next morning when they asked how she had slept, she said, "Scarcely any at all. There was something hard in my bed and I'm black and blue all over my body." Now the prince and his parents knew that she was a real princess because nobody but a real princess could be that sensitive.

You get the idea. Somehow, royalty is supposed to be too delicate, or refined, or something to suffer. How much more should the idea of suffering be foreign to deity? And yet, we get this surprising, even shocking, affirmation that Jesus Christ, God's only Son, who in every way is so superior to human beings, in spite of his divinity, suffered and died.

The Creed tells us specifically that Jesus suffered under Pontius Pilate. The name of Pontius Pilate, the Roman procurator who gave the order to crucify Jesus Christ, fulfills its purpose in the creed by grounding these events in history.

But it is the verbs here that are essential to the theological import of this portion of the Creed: *"suffered, was crucified, dead, buried"*

"Crucified" documents the degrading and torturous mode of suffering that led to Jesus' death, and his death is confirmed by his burial. Unimaginable as these words seem in connection with deity, it is by these words that God's surprising plan for our salvation is marked.

In some ways, the entire incarnation of God's Son can be thought of as suffering. Paul articulates in Philippians 2:6-8 what we all know–that Christ left behind the glory of heaven to take on human form–and not the form of royalty–some elevated human being with special privileges, but the form of a servant. And it was as God's Servant that his only Son carried out God's purpose for the redemption of his people.

We have heard the Scripture text read from Isaiah 52-53, the fourth of Isaiah's "Servant Songs," and that text helps to explain this crucial role of suffering and death that is stated so tersely in the Apostles' Creed.

The first thirty-nine chapters of Isaiah describe the judgment that God will bring upon his people Israel for their failure of servanthood. Israel had been chosen by God and given a mission to reveal God to the world, but Israel had been unwilling or unable to trust God. They had preferred to trust the gods of the nations around them, and Isaiah foresaw that disaster lay ahead.

Nevertheless, Isaiah also foresaw the possibility of the restoration of Israel, and with chapter forty, he begins to address that possibility. Isaiah was confident that God was both able to deliver Israel from the exile that was to come and that he wanted to do so.

Four passages in Isaiah 40-55 are conventionally designated as the "Servant Songs." Together they present a vision of a particular "Servant of Yahweh" or "Suffering Servant" who is entrusted with a special mission on behalf of God's people.

The idea of Israel as God's Servant is not confined to these passages, but in them, and especially in Isaiah 53, there is a new concept of a Servant whose role of vicarious suffering brings healing and deliverance to the people.

It is explicitly Israel who is depicted as God's Servant in these songs, but notably in Isaiah 53, the fourth song, the Servant is portrayed as an individual over against Israel and as suffering on their behalf. This figure was one of those used by New Testament writers to illuminate the mission of Jesus.

The earlier Servant Songs prepare us for the Servant's suffering, but in this last of the Servant songs we are told why the Servant must undergo suffering and degradation. Indeed, the central thought of this text is focused on two great contrasts: 1) the Servant's exaltation and his humiliation and suffering, and 2) what people thought about the Servant and what was really true about him.

The song begins in chapter 52, verse 13, with a description of the exaltation that will come to the Servant. He will be exalted as a result of the deliverance he will bring to his people by his vicarious suffering. Isaiah tells us that as a result of the Servant's wise actions, he "will rise and be lifted up and be highly exalted." He will not remain in his state of humiliation. In reading these words, how can we not think of the exaltation of Christ described in Philippians 2:9-11?

However, no sooner does the prophet affirm the Servant's exaltation than he introduces a contrast by picturing the extent, the depth, of his degradation. As high as his exaltation, so deep was his degradation. Those who looked on the terrible disfigurement of the Servant were appalled and struck with awe, certain that such a terrible judgment had to be punishment for some unspeakable sins the Servant had committed.

His sufferings were so great, his form so disfigured that he no longer resembled a man, yet his disfigurement, which was mistakenly regarded as punishment for his own sins, was rather the condition by which he would bring cleansing to the nations.

As the result of the Servant's amazing suffering, followed by his equally shocking exaltation, the nations will be startled, at a total loss for words, to see this amazing act of God's salvation.

Chapter 53, verse 1 echoes the incredulity of humanity when confronted by such amazing and startling events. The nations will be shocked because they have never before heard of a deliverer who would go to such lengths to save them. But what about those who had heard of this before? Who had believed it?

Who could have thought that when the power of God's arm was revealed, it would not be as the power to crush the enemy, but the power, when the enemy has crushed the Servant, to give back love and mercy?

What image does the "arm of the Lord" bring to your mind? I think of the huge muscled arm of the Vulcan statue that stands over Birmingham, or the arm of the Statue of Liberty in New York harbor, steadily holding aloft its flame. This arm seems puny in comparison; we expect a strong and mighty arm such as conveys visible power.

Even Israel, the people of God who have heard the news and seen the revelation, have refused to believe it. And in human terms, we can understand why they did not believe such a revelation. Isaiah tells us that there was none of the charisma and comeliness that we look for in leaders to distinguish this Servant. Deliverers are supposed to be dominating, forceful, attractive people.

This man fits none of that description. In fact, rather than being drawn to Him, we are repulsed by Him. He shows no outward signs of greatness. Instead of rising up like a mighty oak tree or a cedar of Lebanon, he appears as a sprout, a "sucker," an unwanted shoot that springs up from the root or on the trunk of a tree and is quickly snipped off by the gardener. Or like a tender, young plant struggling for life in dry and barren ground. Such a plant's survival is in doubt from the beginning.

John Oswalt comments: "Isn't it inevitable that we should think of Jesus Christ: a baby born in the back-stable of a village inn. This would shake the Roman Empire? A man quietly coming to the great preacher of the day and asking to be baptized. This is the advent of the man who would be heralded as the Savior of the world? No, this is not what we think the arm of the Lord should be like."[4]

Because the appearance of the Servant fails to meet human expectations of greatness, he is despised—not hated, but regarded of no significance, unworthy of attention. He is rejected by men, though he was himself a man.

But consider what kind of man. He is a man of pain and sickness. What can he do for us? In fact, he makes us uncomfortable.

We don't like to see another person suffering. We think we should do something, but we aren't sure what. We feel guilty for being well. We feel guilty for being glad that we are well. And so, often to avoid the discomfort, we avoid the person. We "hide our faces" from them; we turn away to avoid looking at them.

But was the Servant literally a sick man? Not likely. Rather, because the Servant doesn't fit the stereotype of God's deliverer, he will experience the same avoidance that the sick experience. Such a seemingly insignificant person can hardly

---

[4] John Oswalt, *The Book of Isaiah: Chapters 40-66* in The New International Commentary on the Old Testament (Grand Rapids: William B. Eerdmans Publishing Company, 1998), 382.

be the one to set us free from sin, and so he is discounted, avoided, not even meriting a second thought.

But with verse 4, the prophet takes on our false impressions and again presents a shocking truth: The Servant's sufferings were not his own fault, as "we" thought, but were in fact the result of "our" sins, and resulted in "our" healing.

The force of verses 4-6 brings to the fore the issue of the substitutionary suffering of the Servant. Note the contrast between Him and us: He suffered, but it was we who sinned. The "sorrows" and "suffering" ascribed to the Servant in verse 3, those characteristics that made us "esteem Him not," he is enduring for our weakness and illness. The Servant bears and carries upon Himself the sin sickness that belongs to us.

In the sacrificial rite described in Leviticus, the sacrificial animal carries away the sins of the ones offering the sacrifice so they don't carry them anymore. In like manner, the Servant becomes our substitute. The animal dies in the offeror's place, doing what the offeror must otherwise do. This is the role assigned to the Servant.

And there is a further contrast between the Servant and us. We had thought God was punishing this man for his own sins and failures, but in fact, he was "pierced through" and "crushed" on account of our sins.

Notice the violence and intensity associated with the suffering. "Pierced" and "crushed" convey the idea of the complete destruction of the person in the most painful way possible. This effect shows us how seriously God views our rebellion and sinfulness. We are not guilty of "shortcomings" and "mistakes." Our sins are "the stuff of death and corruption." Unless someone can be found to stand in our place, we are the ones to be pierced and crushed as the result of our own sins.

And the powerful assertion of the prophet is that someone has been found to take on the penalty that was rightfully ours. But, in order for such vicarious suffering to be effective, the Servant who bore it had to be himself one who was utterly free of sin and transgression.

Clearly then, there is only One who could have carried out this mission, Jesus the Christ. And because he took the punishment for our sins, now we can be at peace with God and our healing is complete.

In explaining our sin problem and the reason for the Servant's suffering, the prophet compares us to sheep: we had wandered away from God, heedless of the consequences of our willful actions, much as sheep pursue the next clump of grass, unaware of their tendency to get lost.

And here is the mystery! God has caused the consequences of our sin to fall upon the Servant.

Verse 7 turns the sheep metaphor from us to the Servant. When we are compared to sheep, it is in terms of their tendency to get lost. When the Servant is compared to sheep, it is their non-defensive, submissive nature that is the basis of comparison. Although the Lord ultimately caused the Servant's suffering, the Servant endured that suffering with patience because it was vicarious and voluntary. He offered no self-defense or protest.

How can we read this prophecy and not think of Jesus before the judgment seat of Pilate answering not a word?

Clearly the Servant's suffering was unjust, but not because of a corrupt legal system. It was "the transgressions of my people" (v. 8) that condemned the Servant.

The injustice to the Servant is that he dies the death that God's people should be dying. His death is substitutionary, propitiatory. In reading of this vicarious suffering by the Servant, we inevitably ask "Why?" What is the meaning of this man's suffering in the place of sinners? Why is he doing it? How can he do it?

Verses 10-12 give us the answers. Above all, the prophet asserts, the Servant's tragic story was not an accident of history. It was not the case of a good person in the wrong place at the wrong time. In spite of the appearance that the Servant's suffering and death was at the hands of wicked men, the prophet assures us that it was not. No, it was God's will "to crush him and cause him to suffer."

That, though, seems the worst answer of all. God wanted to crush this man? God wanted him to suffer so terribly? Surely not. Surely the faithful God of the Bible would not bring such bad things on an innocent person. Would he?

Yes, he would if some greater good would be served. What could that greater good possibly be? What could be worth all the terrible things the Servant has endured? The reality is that what God wants to come out of the Servant's suffering is of monumental proportions. God wants human beings to be able to offer this man as "a full and sufficient sacrifice" for all their sins.

This purpose of God is why the Servant could accept what came to him with such submission. He knew that his sufferings came to him from the hand of God, and that God's purpose was a great and good one.

The meaning of the Servant's suffering is found in God's intention that he should become an atoning sacrifice for sin. When the Servant's sacrifice is accepted, two things will happen. In direct contrast to what was said about the Servant in verses 8-9, that he would die without children, his death ending a completely futile life, here the very opposite is said of him. He will see his descendants, he will live a long life, and he will accomplish God's purposes for his life.

So, what has made the difference? One thing: that people accept him as a guilt offering in their place. When that acceptance takes place, his life, far from being futile, will be the most fruitful ever lived. Far from being childless, he will have children in every race on the earth.

The Servant's success is the result of only one thing: his becoming a sacrificial offering. When he does that, the whole process of redemption comes to fruition.

As a result of his suffering and death the Servant accomplishes God's purpose, and he is promised abundant satisfaction. Even as God at creation expressed satisfaction in his handiwork, so the Servant sees the results of his dreadful death and is abundantly satisfied.

The "therefore" of verse 12 reminds us again of Philippians 2:9. In obedience to God's plan, the Servant has descended to the lowest depths. Because of that faithful obedience, God will exalt him to the highest heights. He will have the ultimate victory parade.

The song concludes with a summary of why the Servant is so gloriously exalted. It is because of the Servant's voluntary self-sacrifice, identifying himself with the transgressors, dying their death so that they could live.

In the compelling words of John Oswalt:

> "The Servant will be exalted to the highest heaven not because he was humiliated (although he was), not because he suffered unjustly (although he did), not because he did it voluntarily (although he did), but because it was all in order to carry the sin of the world away to permit God's children to come home to him. He is exalted because he fulfilled God's purpose for his ministry, and that purpose was redemption."[5]

Jesus Christ, God's only Son, *"suffered under Pontius Pilate, was crucified, dead and buried."* Nine succinct but powerful words of the Creed sum up Christ's redemptive work, according to God's plan and purpose.

Such an amazing act of redemption boggles our minds; we can scarcely comprehend it.

Many explanations have been proposed about how the events of September 11, 2001, in New York City, Washington, D.C., and outside Shanksville, Pennsylvania could have happened without U.S. intelligence agencies knowing about them. One person explained: "America suffered not so much from a lack of intelligence as from a lack of imagination."

Our governmental leaders and our intelligence officers simply couldn't conceive of a deed so heinous, so destructive, and so evil. Even now, in the aftermath of that dreadful event, we find ourselves still bewilderingly confronted by the reality of such a seemingly unimaginable act--an unthinkably evil act.

Would to God it were not true.

---

[5] Ibid., 407.

It may seem peculiar and even irreverent to use such an analogy for God's deeds, but I think perhaps it helps us to consider the humanly unimaginable depths of God's love.

In contemplating what God has done for us in Christ, we suffer not so much from a lack of intelligence as from a lack of imagination. We simply cannot conceive of a God whose love is so great that He offers himself as the sacrificial offering for our sins, who suffers the punishment for our transgressions, who will go to any lengths to restore us to relationship with him.

In the aftermath of what Christ has done for us, we find ourselves bewilderingly confronted by the reality of such an unthinkable act.

Not an unthinkably evil act, but an indescribably loving act.

Praise God that it is true!

I preached this sermon in chapel at Beeson Divinity School. The dean chose the Lord's Prayer as our chapel focus for the 2002-2003 school year and assigned faculty members the individual phrases as sermon topics. My assignment was "Hallowed Be Thy name."

God's Reputation at Stake
Matthew 6:9-13
Beeson Divinity School
October 22, 2002

Hallowed be Thy name, Hallowed be Thy name.

In thinking about a title for this sermon, I considered the possibility of using "The Neglected Phrase of the Lord's Prayer" or perhaps, "The Most Overlooked Petition of the Lord's Prayer." I could also have used "The Most Misunderstood Petition of the Lord's Prayer."

In his book, *The God Named Hallowed: The Lord's Prayer for Today*, John Killinger recounts the experience of a family sitting around the table at Sunday dinner. The six year-old, Bobby, seemed lost in thought, tracing designs in his mashed potatoes with a fork.

Suddenly, he poses a question to his parents, "Why don't we call God by his name?"

His parents were understandably puzzled. His mother said, "What do you mean?"

"I mean why don't we call God by his name?"

His mother replied, "I don't understand."

Bobby explained, "In church we always say 'Hallowed be Thy name,' but then we never call him that."

Why don't we call God "hallowed"? Could it be that we don't know what this petition in the Lord's Prayer means? At the least, I suspect we don't give it much thought. We tend to emphasize the "Our Father" and "Thy kingdom come" and we glide right over "Hallowed be Thy Name."

One of my students facetiously told me I should be sure my sermon contained at least ten points that could only be appreciated or understood by drawing on the Greek text. I hope he will forgive me that I only have one Greek lesson to offer as part of this message. To understand the meaning and the intent of the word "hallowed," we need to know a little Greek.

"Hallowed" is the English rendering of the Greek word, *hagiastheto*, which means "to make holy," or more accurately, in this instance, "to treat as holy," for clearly, God's name is already holy—indeed, supremely holy.

The significant feature of this verb is that it is a third person imperative, a form unknown in English. All our imperatives are second person, with the implied "You" pronoun understood in all usages. But in Greek, the third person imperative expresses a request, and to signify that, we generally translate it into English with the words, "let" or "may." For example, "Let your servant now depart in peace; May your name be praised."

This Greek third person imperative is normally used when the speaker is addressing a superior, and in Scripture, we most often find it directed toward God in prayers. And so it is here. But how shall we understand its meaning?

As we have already noted, to pray that God's name be hallowed is not to pray that God may become holy, which he already is, but that he may be treated as holy, that his name should not be despised and profaned by the thoughts and conduct of those who have been created in his image.

That brings us to the next issue: How are we to understand the reference to God's name. God's "name" is a reflection of who God is. God's name represents the nature of God as known through God's self-revelation in history. Holiness, often thought of as "separateness," is less an attribute than what God is. It has to do with the very godhead of God.

In essence, this petition means, "Our Father, cause your eternal nature, revealed in Christ, to be hallowed by us and by all people."

"Hallowed be Thy Name" means approximately the same as "Father, glorify Thy name," as Jesus petitioned in John 12:28. Here the form is passive to indicate that it is God's power that must effect the petition. God is asked to sanctify his name and cause humans to sanctify it. God sanctifies his name by condemning and opposing sin, by separating his people from the world and giving them his commandments and his love and grace. God's people have the task of sanctifying God's name by sanctifying themselves, by keeping God's commandments and doing all other things, and only those things, that bring God glory.

In Ezekiel 36, we read how God's people, Israel, profaned God's name among the nations. Yet, for the sake of his name, his reputation, God promised to sanctify his great name by causing himself to be hallowed before the eyes of the world. God expects no less of us, and this petition of the Lord's Prayer implores God to make us holy. It is to pray, "Grant that I may reverence you. Work in me and others so that we will acknowledge your unsurpassed and glorious holiness always."

But notice that the petition is not expressed in terms of what must happen to us for the prayer to be fulfilled. The highest goal is not that we be made holy; the highest goal is that God's name be hallowed. This removes human beings from the center of the picture, and gives that place to God alone. Humankind—even transformed humankind—is not the chief goal of this universe. As the theologians have told us across the years, the chief end of humans is to glorify God and to enjoy him forever.

So when we speak this petition, we are actually saying, "Lord, may everything I do and say show forth your glory as my Father in heaven, and may all my thoughts be focused on what will bring honor to your name."

This petition rightly balances our approach to God. "Father" invites us into intimate personal relationship, "in heaven" reminds us of God's transcendence, and "hallowed be Thy name" prevents over-familiarity. We do not live in intimacy with God in a way that destroys our reverence for him.

Practically speaking, then, how shall we sanctify God's name? First, we must sanctify God's name in how we think about God. These statements are profoundly instructive for our purposes:

If we think of God on the side of bigness and strength, we make God a bully.

If we imagine that we can avoid the penalty for sin, we slander God's sovereignty.

If we consider ourselves too insignificant for God's notice, we brand God as a celebrity chaser.

If we turn to God only in trouble, we treat God as an ambulance.

How do we think about God? It is a crucial question.

Second, we must hallow God's name in our words. The Jews of old shrank from speaking or writing the name of God, but we tend to use it far too freely—some for a curse or in casual disdain. Cultivating reverence is the best way to conquer blasphemous and careless speech about God. "Out of the abundance of the heart, the mouth speaks." (Matt. 12:34) "From the same mouth come blessing and cursing. Such things ought not to be." (James 3:10)

Third, we must hallow God's name in our daily conduct. We must show reverence for God in our work and in our recreational pursuits. Our business practices, our politics, and our friendships must all honor God's name. How we use our time, our money, our gifts of personality and intellect should all be used to glorify God's name, not our own.

Finally, we must hallow God's name in our worship. This might seem an obvious necessity, but sometimes irreverence shows up where reverence should be most noted. Worship has sometimes become cheap. We present ourselves to God in worship far too casually, treat worship services as informal gatherings of friends, and pay too little attention to the God whose glory we proclaim.

Jesus modeled the prayer he taught us to offer. As he anticipated his upcoming crucifixion, Jesus yet prayed, "Father, glorify your name" (John 12:28). His ultimate goal was that God's name—his character and his nature—

should be recognized and appropriately regarded by all humankind.

"Hallowed be Thy name" is a prayer that, when answered, means that we will hallow God's name. We are asking our heavenly Father to act in such a way that we, and all others, will reverence God and consider God holy in all that we do and say.

At the end of ancient synagogue services, the Jews offered an eschatological prayer, known as the Kaddish. The prayer goes like this:

*"Exalted and hallowed be his great name
in the world which he created according to his will.
May he let his kingdom rule
In your lifetime and in your days and in the lifetime
Of the whole house of Israel, speedily and soon."*

I especially like the way that Phillip Keller in his book, *A Layman Looks at The Lord's Prayer,* expresses this petition: "Father, your reputation is at stake in me today. May I live in such a way as to do Your person great credit. Because of my behavior, may others see You in me, and so honor Your name because of it."

God's reputation is at stake in me today, and in you. Will it be sanctified or will it be profaned?

"Our Father, who art in heaven, hallowed be Thy name."

This sermon I prepared and preached in chapel at Beeson Divinity School. For this occasion, I was allowed to select my own text.

If Possible, Thy Will Be Done
Beeson Divinity School
Matthew 26:36-46
April 6, 2004

Heresy! Is there any word or idea that calls forth a greater anathema for an orthodox Christian? We study the major heresies of the early church and the councils that resolved them in church history, but we rarely hear the term used in modern days. Nevertheless, I was recently shocked to find that I, myself, was thinking about Jesus Christ in a way that at least bordered on the heretical.

I was reading a book whose focus was on the spirituality of Jesus as a model for believers' spirituality. In the early pages, the author spoke of Jesus as a "fellow seeker in the way of faith" who "needed to cultivate his own discipleship and deepen his own understanding of God, the world and his task in life."

My initial reaction to that description was intense—I utterly rejected the idea of Jesus as a seeker needing to grow in spirituality. My reaction was so strong that I turned away from the book, and stopped reading it for several days. But it stayed on my mind and eventually I went back to it, this time with an investigative mind set. Why had it upset me so?

I came to realize that while I affirm intellectually, and by conviction, the two natures of Christ, in practical terms, I thought of Jesus largely, if not entirely, in terms of his divine nature. I was offended by the claims for Jesus' humanity because I related to him in his divinity. I should, perhaps, clarify that this happened before I saw Mel Gibson's movie, *The Passion*.

This startling realization of my unbalanced Christology sent me on a quest to study and learn more about Jesus in his two natures, with emphasis on the human. That journey led me to the gospel account of Jesus in the Garden of Gethsemane on the night before he was crucified.

This experience in the Garden is recorded in all four of the New Testament Gospels, similarly in the Synoptic Gospels and with significant differences in John's Gospel. But I chose Matthew's account particularly because of the way he reports Jesus' prayer: "If it is possible, let this cup be taken from me, yet not as I will, but as you will."

We know the setting: Jesus had a final meal with his disciples, during which he acknowledged Judas as his betrayer and instituted what we still observe as the Lord's Supper. Jesus revealed to his disciples the symbolism of the bread and the wine—his body to be broken, his blood to be spilled as the ultimate sacrificial offering to secure forever reconciliation between God, his Father, and everyone who would believe in him.

When supper was over, Jesus and his now eleven disciples went out to the Mount of Olives to the Garden of Gethsemane. Leaving eight of the disciples near the entrance to the garden, Jesus took his three closest companions, Peter, James and John, with him farther in. There, Matthew tells us, Jesus' demeanor and serene spirit changed as he confessed to these three his anguish and deep sorrow, sorrow almost to the point of death.

And so he asks his three companions to stay awake with him. This word translated "stay awake" doesn't just mean keep your eyes open; it means to remain awake because of the need to be alert and watchful of what is happening. It is the same word Jesus used in his parable describing the need to be watching for the unexpected coming of the Son of Man: "If the owner of the house had known in what part of the night the thief was coming, he would have stayed awake and would not have let his house be broken into (Matt 24:34). Given Jesus' lack of resistance to the arresting party when they arrived, it isn't likely he was instructing the disciples to watch, guarding him against danger, but rather warning them to guard themselves--not physically, but spiritually.

Jesus then went on a little way to pray, and as an expression of his utter dependence upon God, he fell down on the ground to voice his prayer. Jesus, in this time of desperate need, claimed the only relationship able to sustain him for the suffering that awaited him. And there he speaks the words that so poignantly express his humanity: "if it is possible, let this cup—this cup of your righteous wrath over human sin—let this cup be taken from me."

Pause for a moment and let your imagination join mine:

Father, I know what's waiting for me. I've seen the cruelty of the Romans; I've traveled that road beside Golgotha and witnessed the agony of crucifixion. Everything in me is in anguish as I anticipate what the coming hours will bring. And worst of all, I know that in bearing the punishment for all the sins of humanity, in some way you must separate from me. In that experience, I must be cut off from your sustaining presence, and Father, you're all I've got. If there's any other way, if it is possible, spare me from the suffering ahead. But Father, that's my flesh crying out for deliverance—my humanity, and as real as that is, I want more than anything for Your will to be done.

Jesus returned to his three watching companions. Watching? No . . . they are asleep! Can you picture this scene? Here is Jesus, having expressed to these three disciples the depth of his anguish and sorrow, anguish so burdensome it seems it must bring death, and he has poured out his heart to God in prayer asking for deliverance, and the disciples are sleeping.

You see, they are human, too. They didn't comprehend the eminent dangers headed their way. They have eaten well, drunk freely of the wine at dinner, and in the darkness and quiet of Gethsemane, it is natural for them to sleep. I'm afraid I would have been doing the same.

But Jesus knows human nature. Indeed, it is in his humanity that he was wrestling with his own weakness. And he knows that these disciples are about to face their own trials and suffering, and he knows there is only one way they will be strong enough to endure them. So he exhorts them again to stay awake and this time adds the admonition to :pray that you may not come into the time of trial; the spirit indeed is willing, but the flesh is weak."

The temptations and trials that Jesus urges them to avoid are supernatural trials that only God's help will enable humans to avoid or overcome—the kind of trial he is undergoing. For he knows from his own experience that while our human spirits may wish and will to stand firm in faith, obedient to God's will, the flesh is weak, and through the weakness of the flesh, humanity is vulnerable.

Just a short time earlier, during the walk to Gethsemane, all the disciples had followed Peter's lead and firmly attested their intention to stand by Jesus no matter the consequences. But Jesus knew, and events would reveal, that human intentions, no matter how good, are not sufficient for victory in the trials that await them. Indeed, Jesus was urging his disciples to do the same thing he was doing—to battle their fleshly human tendencies by praying for the Father's will to prevail.

When Jesus goes the second time to pray, he uses similar words to those of his first prayer, but this time he reveals acceptance of his path. Again, claiming the intimacy of his relationship to God, he prays, "My Father, if this cup cannot be taken away unless I drink it, your will be done."

He has moved beyond the desperate plea for deliverance that characterized his first prayer, "if it is possible, let this cup pass from me"—to an alignment of his will with the Father's. This "if" might be better understood as "since" this cannot pass unless I drink it, your will be done." Jesus has accepted what he probably knew all along, that his drinking of this cup is indeed his Father's will and way.

A second return to the disciples finds them again sleeping, because, Matthew says, their eyes were heavy. Do you hear the irony? Their eyes were heavy; Jesus' spirit was heavy.

A third retreat for prayer during which Jesus said the same thing as before, and he is ready—strengthened and fortified by his time with his Father. Jesus returns to the disciples with a new energy and resolution. He had committed himself to carry out the Father's will and he prepared himself for what lay ahead. And he goes calmly and confidently to meet the arresting party.

"If it is possible." In some ways those words sound strange coming from Jesus' lips, addressed to his Father. Jesus had repeatedly affirmed in his teaching that with God all things are possible. But here, he was not questioning God's ability; he was petitioning God that if it were possible within God's redemptive plan to accomplish the salvation of human beings without his suffering, he is pleading to be spared. But Jesus never indicates a desire not to accomplish God's will for overcoming human sin. Always, Jesus' prayer was for God's will to be done.

"If it is possible, Your will be done." Yes, Jesus here reveals his humanity. But humanity not controlled by the flesh; controlled by the Holy Spirit. The human spirit is willing. We want God's will to be done; indeed, we want to do it. But our flesh, our humanity, makes us vulnerable to temptation and we are prone to take the easy road when the time of testing comes in the form of hardship and suffering. And so we pray, "Father, if it is possible, let your will be done without my suffering, without my sacrifice, without my pain and struggle."

But accomplishing God's will doesn't work that way. Jesus clearly taught that a servant is not above his master, and that if anyone desired to come after him, they must deny themselves, take up their cross and follow him. You see, God's "Well done, good and faithful servant," comes by way of the cross. And Jesus showed us by putting himself at God's disposal how we as human beings can ensure our faithfulness in the time of trial–through prayer that enables the spirit to triumph over the flesh.

If we understand Jesus' suffering, his passion, as only encompassing the public trials and crucifixion, it is an unrepeatable one-time event. If, however, we include the Gethsemane experience as an important aspect of his passion, it is an experience all Christians can imitate. For at some time in the life of committed Christians there comes the moment of agonizing decision—to obey God and follow his will at great personal cost or to allow Satan to tempt us and lead us to take the easy way out. Because Jesus showed us the way to victory in the agonizing experience of Gethsemane, we, too, can overcome.

Father, if possible, if possible with me—weak, sometimes afraid, even cowardly. I know all things are possible for you, but for me? For you, fellow believer? Yes, for me and for you, because we can do all things through Christ, who strengthens us, even as he was strengthened. "Father, if possible, Your will be done." May it ever be so.

In 2003 Dan Brown published a novel, The Da Vinci Code, *that quickly surged to the top of the bestseller lists worldwide. Its plot line claims that the Merovingian kings of France were descended from the bloodline of Jesus and Mary Magdalene. While it made for a compelling novel, it stirred up a lot of controversy and opposition within Christian denominations. Even though Brown stated in his introduction that the book was fiction, even life-long Christians became confused by it. When my pastor, Gary Furr, invited me to fill the pulpit for him on a Sunday morning, I used the opportunity to address the questions I was being asked about it.*

Who Dares to Speak About Jesus?
2 Timothy 3:1-5, 14-17
Vestavia Hills Baptist Church
July 13, 2004

For over forty weeks Dan Brown's novel, *The Da Vinci Code*, was ranked among the best-selling books on the New York Times bestseller list. By intertwining his fast-paced action thriller with spurious claims about newly discovered information revealing that Jesus was married to Mary Magdalene and the descendants of their children now live in southern France, Brown aroused the interest of millions in thinking about Jesus.

While thinking about Jesus is a good thing, Brown's approach is problematic. He takes a negative view of the Bible and presents a grossly distorted image of Jesus. According to Brown, Christ wasn't even considered divine until the Council of Nicea voted him so in AD 325, and thus he has one of his character's lament that, "Almost everything our fathers taught us about Christ is false."

While Brown is perhaps the best-known and most popular purveyor of such false Christology, he is only the latest of a number of modern voices challenging the traditional biblical account of Jesus. For example, every year around Easter and Christmas, the media find it expedient to feature some acknowledgment of Jesus Christ as the historical figure associated with these events. At such times, they turn not to evangelical Bible-believing theologians for their authorities, but to the notorious Jesus Seminar.

This group of scholars initially gathered in 1985, embarked on the unprecedented project of examining available sources—biblical and nonbiblical—to discover "what Jesus really said." Such a quest, by its stated intent, indicates that Seminar participants do not believe the gospel accounts about Jesus. They reason that it is impossible for the Gospels to be historically accurate because they record things that simply can't happen, such as people coming alive again after dying and food multiplying—miracles, in other words.

They would argue that we live in a closed universe of natural order, with God (if there is a God) locked out of the system. If miracles can't happen, the reports in the New Testament must be fabrications. Therefore, the Gospels are not historical. As a result of applying these presuppositions to their analysis of the Gospels, the Seminar has concluded that only 18 percent of the sayings attributed to Jesus were actually uttered by him. As an example, they conclude that the only part of the Lord's Prayer we can reasonably affirm as authentic to Jesus are the two words, "Our Father."

Perhaps the best summary of the approach of this group is voiced by retired bishop of the Newark, New Jersey Diocese, John Shelby Spong, who says the birth narrative about Jesus should not be taken literally and that the resurrection was not an actual historical event. According to Spong: "Christianity desperately needs to escape the language of antiquity that has portrayed sacrifice and shed blood as signs of salvation . . .. The Jesus who "died for our sins' has simply got to go in our post-Darwinian world."

Such secular approaches to Jesus abound in our world, and as these voices bombard us from many sources and multiple directions, even self-identified Bible-believing Christians can find it difficult to sort out the truth.

It is interesting that these contemporary voices present their views as if they were something new. Actually, false belief and false teaching about Jesus has been an issue for Christianity from its earliest days. We should not be surprised, and we need not be confused. The apostle Paul in his second letter to Timothy instructs him about how to deal with false teaching, which was infecting the church at Ephesus during the first century. His guidance for Timothy is equally valid for us today.

The text for this message is found in the third chapter of 2 Timothy, verses 1-5 and 10-17. Paul wrote two letters to Timothy in Ephesus where Paul had left him as his representative because Paul had discovered false teaching going on there. Paul needed to travel on to Macedonia, but he was greatly concerned about the problems the Ephesian church was experiencing and young Timothy's ability to withstand the pressures of these false teachers and ideas. Therefore, he wrote letters to Timothy encouraging him and exhorting him to faithfulness.

In this second letter, Paul felt a sense of heightened urgency because he was once again imprisoned in Rome, and this time, had little hope of getting out alive. Indeed, this second letter to Timothy is the last extant letter of Paul that we have, and in it, he instructed Timothy in how to carry on the work of the gospel after Paul's death.

At the beginning of chapter three, Paul reminded Timothy that he should not be surprised that he and the church were undergoing hardship, for he says such things are expected "in the last days." This idea was a common motif in Jewish apocalyptic thought and was picked up by Jesus (Mark 13:3-23). The early church saw the increase of evil as evidence that the end had already begun.

Although we may have a tendency to think of the last days as the time immediately preceding the return of Christ, according to biblical usage, the last days had dawned with the first coming of Christ. Thus, Peter at Pentecost, explaining the phenomenal manifestation of the Holy Spirit quotes the prophet, Joel, that "in the last days" God would pour out his Spirit on all flesh (Acts 2:14-17). Similarly, the Letter to the Hebrews begins with the assertion that God who formerly had spoken through the prophets has "in these last days" spoken to us through his Son (1:2). So Timothy was already living in the last days, and we are still living in them.

Note also that the "distressing times" were the result of peoples' values. Verses 2-4 enumerate a variety of vices, but the key to all of them is found in the "lover" expressions at the beginning and end of the list. "People will be lovers of themselves . . . lovers of pleasure rather than lovers of God" (v. 4). It is humanity, individual persons and people collectively, who are responsible for the hard times the church has to bear—people whose behavior is self-centered and godless.

Adding to the distress is that these false teachers are claiming to speak from a position of godliness; they claim to speak authoritatively about Jesus and life in Christ. They claim the authority of the church—John Shelby Spong is a bishop; members of the Jesus Seminar hold church affiliations and positions as teachers of Christian Scripture.

But their teaching proves that they don't understand the power of true godliness; they only claim its outward form. Timothy is charged to avoid them! Their teaching can be infectious and their diseased thinking is dangerous to healthy belief. Timothy is told to stay away from them just as he would keep away from someone carrying a physical infection.

In the following verses, Paul specifically applies his description of those causing distress to the false teachers in Ephesus, and then offers up his own conduct and teaching to Timothy for contrast with them. Bringing the message home to Timothy, personally, in verse 14 Paul writes, "But as for you . . ." clearly indicating that Timothy's belief and manner of life should provide a contrast to the false teachers.

In other words, Paul is saying, "Timothy, here is a description of those false to Christ and sound teaching about him, but you must not be like them." Rather, Paul says, you are to "continue in what you have learned and firmly believed" for two very significant reasons: 1) you know from whom you learned the truths you have believed in. Paul himself had been Timothy's teacher, following and building upon the instruction in Scripture by Timothy's mother and grandmother since his infancy. Paul had proven by his life that he was confident of his belief in Christ, and Timothy had trusted him. And 2) what he had learned from Paul was consistent with the Scriptures he had studied since childhood.

Timothy had two reasons to remain loyal to what he firmly believed: because he had learned it from the Scriptures, and from trusted, godly teachers. These same grounds hold true for us today. We have the testimony of God's prophets in the Old Testament and the testimony of the apostles in the New Testament. We have the godly voices of two thousand years of church history and the trusted teachers and preachers who have passed on to us the gospel message.

The message and lives of our teachers we know from experience, which tells us if we can trust them. Paul invited Timothy to examine his life and witness as the assurance that he was a trustworthy teacher. In regard to Scripture, he offered two fundamental truths to support its trustworthiness. First, its origin—it comes from God. It is "God-breathed," brought into existence by the Spirit of God. Paul offers no theory or explanation of inspiration here; he simply attests to his own and the Church's belief. It originated in God's mind and was communicated by God's breath or Spirit. It is therefore rightly termed "the Word of God" for God spoke it.

The second truth about Scripture is its purpose: it is profitable (useful, beneficial) both for correct belief and for correct conduct. Concerning belief, it is profitable for teaching the truth and for refuting error. As for conduct, it is profitable for reformation of behavior and discipline in right living. Scripture is God's chief instrument for bringing those who belong to God into maturity, that they may be fully qualified, equipped for every good work.

Who dares to speak about Jesus? In our day, as in days of old, many voices dare to do that very thing. Some are trustworthy voices, some are not. So how can we know whom to trust? Paul affirms that the sacred writings, the Christian Scriptures, provide us with the reliable guide for our instruction and our conduct. In Peter's second letter to the churches in Asia Minor, he confirms Paul's claim. In chapter 1:3-4 he states: "His [God's] divine power has given us everything needed for life and godliness, through the knowledge of him who called us by his own glory and goodness. Thus he has given us, through these things, his precious and very great promises, so that through them you may escape from the corruption that is in the world."

We all have a choice: What will be our source of authority? Whose voice will we listen to? Will it be the secular voices of popular culture and the trends of the day or will it be the God-breathed, time-tested Word of God? Will we allow culture to critique the Bible or will we use the Bible to critique culture? Paul was confident of our inability to do both, for in Romans 12:2 he says, "Do not be conformed to this world but be transformed by the renewing of your minds so that you may discern what is the will of God—what is good and acceptable and perfect."

Jesus has many interpreters today. Paul's charge to Timothy is still God's charge to us: Continue in what you have learned and firmly believed as attested in the sacred writings, for by them we "may escape the corruption that is in the world."

During the fall semester 2005, I was on sabbatical leave, doing research on racial reconciliation for the Church. A requirement of that leave was that upon my return to Beeson in the spring I would preach a sermon related to my sabbatical activity. This message is the one I delivered for that occasion.

I Press On
Philippians 3: 7-16
Beeson Divinity School
April 18, 2006

> *"I'm pressing on the upward way,
> new heights I'm gaining every day;
> but still I'll pray till heaven I've found,
> Lord, lead me on to higher ground."*
> —Johnson Oatman, Jr.

Yes, my friends, I am pressing on, I press on.

I don't do this as if it were something new or unique to me. No, I'm following the example of the Apostle Paul, my ancestor in the faith.

In this text from Paul's letter to the Christians at Philippi, Paul explains to those dear saints that even though he is Christ's personally commissioned ambassador, and even though he has been blessed with amazing insights and revelations from God the Father, and even though his path is always guided by the Holy Spirit, Paul himself has not attained to a perfect knowledge or experience of God.

Paul knows that until the time of his homegoing and the final consummation of his salvation, he cannot attain to full and perfect knowledge of God. His humanity won't allow it. But at the same time, Paul knows that God wants to give him all that he, Paul, can possibly absorb. And Paul wants it all. He has tasted and seen that the Lord is good and faithful and gracious and loving, and he wants his life saturated with those qualities.

And so, Paul does what he can do . . . he presses on. He actively pursues those good gifts of God. He says I know I can't have it all right now, but I always want more, and so I am giving myself to the pursuit of what God wants to give me.

He tells us that the reason he wants to make all God's gifts a part of himself is because God has already made Paul a part of himself. In verse 12 he says, "I press on to make it my own, because Christ Jesus has made me his own." It is as if Paul is saying, "Jesus has taken hold of my life and shown me how much more it can be than what I can make of it. He empowers me to get more and more of himself into me, and I'm going for it."

Like the runner who competes in a race, Paul says I'm not wasting time with looking backward, either with regret or triumph, lest that deter me from the goal toward which I'm running. No, I'm running with my face forward, eyes on the prize, straining toward what lies ahead. Every muscle, every nerve, every fiber of my being, stretching, straining, reaching for the goal—the prize of the upward call of God in Christ Jesus.

Paul says, in effect, "God has laid hold on me, and claimed me as his own son, and being the loving Father that he is, he has a storehouse of good things he wants to give me. And I've sampled the goodness of this Father and it is beyond the best blessings I could imagine, and I want more. I'm determined to get more of his goodness into me."

I wonder if Paul had seen into the throne room of God as we are privileged to do in the book of Revelation. Paul said that he had ascended into the third heaven, so maybe God had given him a vision of what to expect when his life on earth was finally ended and he was privileged to be in the eternal presence of God.

I hope so, because that vision of the heavenly throne room shows us what God has in store for us. Consider this description of God's throne room found in Revelation 7:9-10: "After this I looked, and behold, a great multitude that no one could number, from every nation, from all tribes and peoples and languages, standing before the throne and before the Lamb, clothed in white robes, with palm branches in their hands, and crying out with a loud voice, "Salvation belongs to our God who sits on the throne, and to the Lamb!"

Did you notice all those people whose voices are united in proclaiming the praises of our Lord? Persons from every nation, tribe, people and language. That means people of every ethnic group, people of every color, people of every culture . . . people in all their richly created diversity . . . joined together—get that? "Together"!

If God's best intention and ultimate desire for us is that we who are all members of his family should be "together" in heaven, why not start preparing for that now? Even now, we have the means and opportunity to be together with our brothers and sisters of every nation, tribe, people, and language. We are family already because we belong to God. Why don't we claim that kinship by being in loving relationship with one another now? Why do we separate ourselves from those of different skin color or different culture or different ethnicity when they are our family members?

You know that one of the distinguishing characteristics of Paul's theology is his "already/not yet" perspective on God's redemptive work among us. There are aspects of God's final intention for his people and his world that are not yet operative. But on the other hand, we do have available to us NOW certain dimensions of what will ultimately be ours. We have a foretaste of the world to come because of the finished work of Christ and God's Holy Spirit indwelling us.

What sense does it make to say to God, "Well, I'll just wait until the final consummation to avail myself of these blessings you have in store for me; no need to enjoy them now"? Does that make sense? Which of us is not into instant gratification? We are a people known for wanting what we want and wanting it NOW! Don't we want all that God has for us? Don't we want as much of it as we can get now?

Paul tells us in Ephesians 3 that God's manifold wisdom has willed that through the church it might be shown to all the world that God's plan always intended for all peoples, regardless of race, ethnicity, skin color, or any other distinctive trait, to be "members of the same body and partakers of the promise in Christ Jesus through the gospel" (v. 6).

How foolish of us to reject the manifold wisdom of God!

Paul says God has revealed this wise plan now because God intends for the people who call themselves the family of God to begin implementing this plan. So it is our job as the church to be the advance unit of what God wants his creation to be: a unified people, bringing him glory, drawn from all languages, nations, peoples, and tongues.

Remember Jesus saying, "Unto whom much is given, of that one much will be required" (Luke 12:48)? We as believers have been given much, including a vision of God's future for us, and that brings obligation.

So I ask another series of questions:

How can I refuse to be in relationship with my brothers and sisters of color?

How can I stand silent and unfeeling when my black brothers and sisters are afraid to drive in a nearby city because of the prejudice based on their skin color?

How can I stand silent when my black brothers and sisters are denied housing and quality schooling because of their skin color?

How can I stand silent when my black brothers and sisters are denied jobs and promotions because they are black?

My list of questions could go on and on, but you get the point.

My sisters and brothers, such things ought not to be.

So how do we as the redeemed people of God work to be reconciled with our brothers and sisters in God's family who are different from us in some way?

I think we have to begin by acknowledging that there are no easy answers. Racial reconciliation is hard work. It requires us to be more like Jesus and less like the rest of our society. But most of us are creatures of conformity, and it is difficult for us to be counter-cultural, to swim against the current. And yet, isn't that what Jesus' radical call to discipleship is all about—to shun the broad and popular path and to follow him on the narrow and difficult way?

Making the assumption that we all WANT to live as God would have us to, let's look at some particulars.

First of all, we white folks have to acknowledge our own complicity in the structures of racism. Joseph Barndt, a pastor in the Bronx in New York City, argues that "racism in the United States is not only an issue between Blacks and whites, it is an issue of power, domination, and control that defines white America's relationship with Native Americans, Hispanics, and Asian Americans."[6]

The reality is that "whites have benefited from the structure of racism whether they have ever committed a racist act, uttered a racist word, or entertained a racist thought. Just as surely as African Americans and people of color suffer in a white society because they are African Americans, Native Americans, Hispanics, Asians, whites benefit because they are white."[7]

Listen to The Reverend Al Miles writing on racism in Hawaii:

I'm always suspicious of any white person who claims to fully understand. . . .. It's been my experience that most whites don't have a clue as to what racism feels like on a deep personal level. Many whites are intellectually and morally sensitive to the problem. Some have even suffered a degree of discrimination. But their race is treated as superior, not placed in an inferior position like many other racial groups. When one comes from a position of power and superiority, as do whites, it is nearly impossible to internalize the feelings of those who have lived under constant oppression simply because of their racial heritage. And

---

[6] Joseph Barndt. *Dismantling Racism* (Minneapolis: Augsburg, 1991), viii.
[7] Ibid., ix.

besides, who would want to internalize these feelings? Racism feels awful.[8]

Just to be confessional for a minute, this was a hard idea for me to accept. I reasoned that I harbored no ill will toward persons whose skin or ethnicity or culture was different from mine. I had not treated such persons any differently than I treated white persons. In truth, I had always been appalled and ashamed of those aspects of my American history that had led to the mistreatment of all those groups. My heart went out to them. I considered myself guiltless, "clean" if you will, on the issue of racism.

But over time, I came to realize that even if my ancestors had not owned slaves, even if they had not driven Native Americans from their lands nor gathered Asian Americans into concentration camps, I have benefited from the privileges and powers that are the result of those actions, simply because my skin is white. And I have no control over the color of my skin, but by my participation, without protest, in the society that affords me privileges and rights because of my skin color, I collude in the effects of a racist system.

I don't know how that strikes you, but it doesn't make me feel good. I don't want to be treated better—or worse—than my brothers and sisters, especially for characteristics we have no control over. So one of the most important steps in overcoming racism is for white people to recognize "our own unknowing complicity in the institutional aspects of racism and summoning up the will to challenge the status quo in our immediate surroundings." To a large extent, racism is a white problem because to be maximally effective, change has to take place within the white community.

---

[8] Curtiss Paul DeYoung. *Reconciliation: Our Greatest Challenge—Our Only Hope* (Valley Forge: Judson Press, 1997), 151.

It is important to realize that "every church and each individual Christian in America today communicates a great deal about the relevance of salvation in Jesus Christ to racial reconciliation and whether God has endowed his children with any special gift that can heal the racial divisions separating people."

Jim Lo, an Asian American college professor and former missionary to South Africa and Cambodia, cogently expresses the challenge facing us as Christians:

> *In obedience to God, the Church in North America must choose acceptance of, and cultural sensitivity to, those from different ethnic backgrounds. If that is to happen, it must begin with individual Christians—like you—[and me]—who are willing to move out of their comfort zones and intentionally create relationships with people of other cultures.*

As Christians we must press on toward the prize for the upward call of God in Christ Jesus. We MUST be agents of racial reconciliation. Racial reconciliation is not an option for Christians; it is part of our calling in the family of God.

Racial reconciliation will not happen of its own accord. If we want to live now in the community of faith that God intends for us for all eternity, we must pursue racial reconciliation intentionally. We must make the effort to form relationships with our brothers and sisters of a different color. We must learn to understand and appreciate their culture, their fears, their strengths and values. We must stop trying to make them like us; we must love them for who they are.

We will make mistakes; we will offend because of ignorance and insensitivity; we will need to be forgiven, again and again; we will need to persevere.

My friends, I am pressing on. I am straining forward toward the prize—to claim all that God has in mind for me, especially that loving, family relationship with ALL my sisters and brothers in Christ. I pray that you will join me on the journey.

With occasional exceptions, my pastor tends to follow the lectionary for his sermon texts. He was doing so in the summer of 2006 when he asked me to preach for him on a Sunday morning in July, and I chose to follow his lead by using a lectionary text.

The Sufficiency of Grace
2 Corinthians 12:2-10
Vestavia Hills Baptist Church
Sunday, July 9, 2006

When the apostle Paul wrote what we know as the second letter to the Corinthians, he was experiencing a tumult of emotions. On the one hand, he felt relief and joy because the majority of believers in the Corinthian church had responded favorably to his latest corrective and reaffirmed their confidence in his apostleship.

On the other hand, he felt anger and concern because a stubborn minority of rebellious church members was continuing to discount his authority because Paul's opponents influenced them. Out of this jumble of emotions Paul wrote 2 Corinthians both to encourage those who were loyal and to, once more, call upon the resistors to turn back.

You are likely familiar with Paul's tempestuous relationship with this Corinthian church. He had founded it on his second missionary journey and had spent some eighteen months there making converts and teaching the believers. Even after he left Corinth to return to Jerusalem, he continued as their "father" in the faith.

Some three years after leaving Corinth, when Paul had embarked on his third missionary journey and was established in Ephesus, he wrote the letter we know as 1 Corinthians in response to reports he had received of some attitudes and activities in the Corinthian church that were not consistent with Christian behavior.

Paul also sent Timothy to visit the Corinthians on his behalf, but when Timothy returned he reported that the problems continued and, in fact, had escalated due to the recent appearance in Corinth of opponents of Paul from outside the city. These opponents sought to undermine Paul's gospel and Paul's authority as an apostle by pointing out his weaknesses. They wanted to establish their own authority by boasting of their accomplishments and credentials.

The first century outlook in Corinth was not all that different from what we see in America today. A person's standing in the community, their prestige and influence, were based upon external measures of success. The accumulation of wealth, the wearing of expensive and beautiful clothes, and the ability to speak articulately and persuasively were prime evidences of personal power and elevated status. Paul had none of those things. And so, as his opponents began their campaign to undermine his authority and status in the church, they pointed out Paul's lack and promoted their own superiority in spirituality, rhetoric, and personal presence.

Paul sent a stern letter of reprimand to the church by Titus and then anxiously awaited Titus' return to learn of the church's reaction. When Paul met up with Titus he learned that the response was mixed—the majority had reaffirmed their loyalty to Paul, but a small minority remained stubbornly resistant.

Paul needed to express his elation and gratitude for those who had reaffirmed their loyalty to him. He wanted them to be further strengthened in their commitment to the true gospel, upon which their church had been founded. At the same time, he recognized the dangers that threatened the health and wellbeing of this church if some of its members continued to follow in the false value system of his opponents.

By the time we get to chapter twelve, Paul had finished with his praise and appreciation for the faithful and is well into the confrontation of his opponents. Knowing that he had to engage them on the basis of their perceived values, he felt it necessary to counter their boasting about themselves with his own grounds for boasting. Therefore, Paul asserted his own ethnic and religious credentials—Hebrew, descendant of Abraham, minister of Christ. In all of these areas, he had the greater reason to boast, especially in terms of his sufferings for the sake of the gospel. Paul despises the necessity of boasting in order to be convincing, and contrary to his opponents, who insist on boasting of their achievements and evidences of power, Paul says that he prefers to boast about his weaknesses.

When we get to the text we are focusing on today, Paul comes to the climax of his argument. He says let's look at spiritual evidences of superiority. Let's talk about visions and revelations of the Lord, the highest manifestations of God's approval and of divine insights. He says I know a man who was taken up by God into the highest realm of heaven, into Paradise itself where God dwells, and was told things by God that are so lofty God won't allow them to be spoken of on earth.

Paul's reluctance to boast about such experiences is evidenced by his speaking of this event in the third person—"I know a man . . .." When we get to verse 7, however, it is obvious Paul is speaking of himself, for lest he "get the big head" over being so blessed and privileged by God, God sent him a thorn in the flesh to keep him mindful of his weakness.

You see an out-of-the-ordinary spiritual experience, just as an out-of-the-ordinary secular experience, can become the basis of self-important boasting. Without the thorn as a constant reminder of his frailty, Paul, being only human, would have been tempted to boast or brag about how special he was to God—why else would God have given him such an exceptional experience? God must consider him a cut above the average believer since such encounters are rare. You see the danger?

We don't know what the exact nature of Paul's thorn was. A lot of speculation has gone on about it, but since it specifies "in the flesh," it was most likely some sort of physical impairment, perhaps one that was visible to others as well as to Paul. It isn't important what it was; in fact, it's probably good that we don't know because it allows us to apply Paul's situation to the variety of afflictions that God allows his children to undergo.

What is important to note is that while the thorn was Satan's work, it was God who allowed it. Just as God had permitted and enabled Paul's rapture to the third heaven, God was the one who allowed the thorn. God knew that the thorn was what was needed to keep Paul from becoming conceited about his heavenly experience.

But note that Paul did not enjoy the thorn in his flesh. He was no masochist or martyr who sought suffering and hardship thinking those somehow made him more worthy. No, Paul prayed for the removal of that thorn. Just as Jesus pleaded for the removal of the cup of his suffering in Gethsemane, Paul asked God to take it away. But, just as God lovingly said no to Jesus in Gethsemane, he said no to Paul. The prayer was answered, but not in the way requested. There is a profound truth for us here about prayers to which God says no. These answers that appear to be negative are ultimately positive, because somehow they bring God's blessing.

God's answer to Paul's prayer came in the form of an explanation and is the high point of the entire letter. "My grace is sufficient for you, for my power is made perfect in weakness." Notice that God doesn't say, "My power is sufficient; my will is sufficient; your stoic bearing of this pain is sufficient." He says, "My grace is sufficient;" my grace is all that you need, for this and for all life's trials.

Imagine God saying, "In your weakness, my power can most effectively be manifest. Because Paul, if you do your ministry out of your power, people see you, and lift you up. But if they see your weakness, yet see powerful ministry coming forth from you, they have to know it comes from a source greater than yourself. It is not human ability, but my sovereign power that works in and through you."

And Paul's response to that is an unequivocal, "Yes, Lord!" So he says, let me boast NOT about the things that impress the world with me, but let me glory in the things that show my weakness because then the world will see the power of Christ and be drawn to him.

What are you doing with your thorn? Many, if not all of us, have them, you know. Maybe yours, like Paul's, is a physical limitation; maybe it's a spiritual issue; perhaps it's a relationship that's troubled; or an attitude that pricks and scars, others as well as ourselves.

Have you asked God to remove it? Or fix it? Yet it lingers on. Have you listened to hear if God is telling you to surrender your thorn to his grace, to allow him to use your suffering to conform you more to the likeness of Jesus

Christ? God's word to Paul two thousand years ago may well be his word to us today. Remember that suffering is the way of the cross. Don't kick against the pricks, but surrender them to my grace and experience my sufficiency for dealing with your difficulty.

God's grace. We throw that word around too loosely sometimes. Most of us can quote the canned definition of grace we learned years ago in Sunday School or Vacation Bible School—God's unmerited loving favor. The preacher Phillips Brooks explained GRACE with an acrostic: G-R-A-C-E = God's Riches at Christ's Expense.

God assured Paul, as he would assure us, that his grace is sufficient, but do we really claim it for our lives? Are we allowing God's grace to sustain us and conform us to the likeness of Jesus Christ, even as his grace has provided for our salvation? John Owen, the great Puritan theologian once said, "Raise your expectations of what Christ can do for you." Do we need to raise our expectations of God's grace?

Consider these words from a sermon preached on this text by Charles Spurgeon in 1876:

It is easy to believe in grace for the past and for the future, but to rest in it for the immediate necessity is true faith . . . . At this moment, and at all moments which shall ever occur between now and glory, the grace of God will be sufficient for you. This sufficiency is declared without any limiting words, and therefore I understand the passage to mean that the grace of our Lord Jesus is sufficient to uphold you, sufficient to strengthen you, sufficient to comfort you, sufficient to make your trouble useful to you, sufficient to enable you to triumph over it, sufficient to bring you out of it, sufficient to bring you out of ten thousand like it, sufficient to bring you home to heaven. Whatever would be good for you, Christ's grace is sufficient to bestow; whatever would harm you, his grace is sufficient to avert; whatever you desire, his grace is sufficient to give it to you if it is good for you; whatever you would avoid, his grace can shield you from it if so his wisdom shall dictate . . . .. Here let me press upon you the pleasing duty of taking home the promise personally at this moment, for no believer here need be under any fear, since for you also, at this very instant, the grace of the Lord Jesus is sufficient.

This morning we are going to commemorate in Holy Communion the most incredible manifestation of God's grace—his saving grace in the life, death, and resurrection of his Son, Jesus Christ. As we partake of the Lord's Supper and celebrate our union with Jesus Christ, and with one another as his body, let me encourage you to reflect anew and embrace with gratitude God's amazing and all-sufficient grace.

From 2003 to 2005, I participated in The Upper Room's Academy for Spiritual Formation. In 2010, I was privileged to serve on the leadership team for a 5-Day Academy, sponsored by the Cooperative Baptist Fellowship. As a member of the team, I was assigned to prepare and deliver a sermon for one of the evening services of "Word and Table." This sermon I developed on an assigned text for that occasion.

Wade in the Water
Exodus 14:10-14
St. Ignatius Retreat House
Atlanta, Georgia
April 2010

Water—with two-thirds of the earth's surface covered by water and the human body consisting of 75 percent water, it's clear that water is one of the prime elements responsible for life on earth. Water circulates through the land just as it does through the human body, transporting, replenishing, and carrying away waste material.

In addition to these physical and biological functions, water has been used since antiquity as a symbol for expressing devotion and purity. Some cultures, such as the ancient Greeks, went as far as to worship what they thought were gods who lived in and commanded the waters.

Similarly, water is one of the most significant images in our Christian Scriptures. It is used for washing, for ritual cleansing, and for drinking. Both God and Christ are often associated with water—as the source of living water or as a means of judgment. Symbolically, water is associated with personal affliction, with cleansing from sin, and with the

Holy Spirit. And when we think redemptively, the water of baptism is the most profound of water symbols.

Thus, the title assigned for today's message, "Wade in the Water," is pregnant with spiritual implications. In its origins as a Negro spiritual emerging out of slavery times, this overtly biblical song carried the encoded message to runaways that they should wade in the water of streams and creeks along their journey to thwart the efforts of bloodhounds sniffing out their path. It wasn't enough just to run away and stay on relatively safe, dry ground; they had to be willing to risk the cold water of flowing streams and the slippery rocks or shifting sands of the stream bed if they were to succeed in their flight.

It shouldn't be difficult then to link the words of that old spiritual with our Scripture text for today from Exodus 14, which recounts the beginning of the flight of the Hebrews from slavery in Egypt. Scripture tells us that when Pharaoh let the people go, God led them toward the Red Sea. But Pharaoh, after letting the people go, changed his mind. So Pharaoh had his chariot made ready, rounded up his army, and they pursued the Israelites, overtaking them where they were camped by the sea. It is at this point we take up the story.

Of course, we know what happened. God caused the waters of the Red Sea to be rolled up like a wall, and the Hebrews went through the water on dry ground. But when the Egyptians pursued them and got into the middle of the sea, God caused the waters to come rushing back together, and Pharaoh and all his army were destroyed.

Now it might seem to you that this recounting of the Israelites' escape from Egypt and Pharaoh is interesting from a salvation history perspective. And you might think it's instructive for reminding us of God's sovereignty over all the created order, but you might think this story has little application to our lives in the twenty-first century. But, let's take a closer look.

The Israelites had felt the restrictions and limitations of life as slaves in Egypt. They knew life is hard, work is daily, and there is not much to relieve the monotony. But they believed in God and they believed he knew about them and wouldn't always let them suffer. They cried out to God for relief, for deliverance. And one day along came Moses with awesome demonstrations of God's power at his command.

They experienced God's miracles, they listened to Aaron's inspired oratory, and finally, they were persuaded that God really was acting for their deliverance. And so they made ready to leave, and they marched out boldly. We can imagine their thoughts, "Whew, that was really something! God persuaded Pharaoh to let us go without a fight, and we are out of there! No more slavery in Egypt for us! Let the celebration begin!" Can't you just imagine their amazement and incredulity that this escape from Egypt was really happening? There was joy all around.

And then, they looked up, and here came the Egyptians—marching out after them in battle array with their chariots and their weapons. Suddenly their rejoicing and celebrating turned to terror. And as frightened people so often do, they turned on their leader. They lambasted Moses: "Why didn't you let us die in Egypt? At least there we could expect to die a somewhat natural death. As bad as that was, it would have been better than dying violently out here in the desert, all of us in one great massacre."

But Moses was a leader prepared. Whatever terrors might have been raging inside of him, he took the part of the courageous leader God had prepared him to be, and he spoke confidently to the people: "Don't be afraid. Stand firm." And God's response to the people's cries is instructive: "Why are you crying out to me? Tell the Israelites to move on."

God had promised to go with them, he had shown himself strong on their behalf, and yet they were fearful and cried out in despair when they felt threatened.

You see, it's one thing to say we believe in God and that we trust him, but it's another thing to follow him to the edge of all the light we have and take one more step into the unknown. We like to see the path ahead clearly and with plenty of light shed on it, but generally that isn't God's way. The Israelites were caught up in the thrill of deliverance and hadn't stopped to think or envision what the journey to freedom would involve.

Suppose they had known beforehand that God was planning to guide them toward an uncrossable body of water. Suppose they had insisted that, before they left Egypt, scouts should be sent out in advance to report back that the way was clear, the Red Sea parted and waiting. If they had, they would have remained slaves.

No one knew what God was going to do to rescue the Israelites from pursuit by the Egyptians. They could only trust that God was going to do something. But they didn't do so well when they saw nothing had been prepared in advance—at least, nothing they could see. There were no bridges, no boats, only water in front and an army behind.

Do you see the principle of spiritual life this story depicts? God told them to act on what they already knew of him. He said, "Stop crying out in despair, and move forward in faith." The water was parted only after they acted in faith and obeyed God's instruction. God gave them no advance plans. He only gave them himself. God was the plan.

Can you identify with the Hebrew people? I can. How many times have I seen God's faithfulness to me across the years, and yet in times of crisis, I wring my hands, cry out, and scramble to escape through my own weak and ineffective means.

Do you, like the Hebrews, and like me, have no reason ever to doubt God's power and provision because you've experienced it over and over again? And do we, also like the Hebrews, when confronted by crisis, cry out to God as if we're helpless to overcome it? How foolish we are! We're not helpless, just as the Hebrews weren't helpless, because the Lord fights for us, just as he did for them.

I confess that at various times in my journey, I have found courage by reading this very text. I have found strength and fortitude to go forward by remembering that the God who parted the waters for the Hebrews and who fed them in the wilderness is the same God I serve. If I am following his will, he will make the way for me.

Do you wrestle with surrendering your life, your ministry, to God's care? Do you go about your life anxious and fretful over situations that seem insurmountable, over relationships that seem broken beyond any hope of repair, over discontentment with your life circumstances and prospects? Do you as a pastor, despair because your church isn't growing deeper with Christ, doesn't seem to have the vision of a missional church? Maybe you, like me, need to immerse yourself in a time of remembrance—remembering God's faithful provision for you in the past, remembering God's faithful provision for the Hebrew people.

Such remembering transforms our anxiety into assurance. Our way will never be without its valleys, our life never without hardship and challenge. But Jesus has promised to be with us always, just as God was always with his people. Our God is the same yesterday, today, and forever.

So wade in the water. Take that step of faith, one step beyond the light and into the darkness, trusting that God will make your way sure. He likely won't tell you ahead of time how he's going to do it or what you're going to face on the journey. But he does give you the assurance that he goes with you and before you and his power is sovereign over all the earth. Wade in the water and watch for the seas to part.

This is another Sunday morning sermon for my church congregation on a text from the Lectionary.

A Close Encounter of the Divine Kind
Genesis 32:22-31
Vestavia Hills Baptist Church
July 31, 2011

This morning's text narrates a significant episode in the Old Testament narrative about Jacob, one of the ancient patriarchs in God's redemptive plan. In this passage we find Jacob en route back to Canaan after his sojourn among his mother's relatives in the land of Paddan Aram.

What an amazing story!—this narrative about Jacob's wrestling with God in the night! This would be a remarkable story under any circumstances, but that it happens to Jacob is especially stunning.

Jacob was a son of Isaac, grandson of Abraham, chosen by God to be a link in the family of promise. But Jacob seems so unlikely a candidate to be the bearer of God's promises to Abraham, at least to our way of thinking. Jacob was a notorious "bad boy" of the Bible. You know the stories. He was born a twin to his brother, Esau, but Jacob was the second born, and therefore the younger son. But he was definitely not the weaker son. His very name, Jacob, means "heel-grabber," and it ominously foretold his nature as a deceiver, one who takes from another through scheming.

As these sons of Isaac grew to manhood, we learn that Esau is an outdoorsman, a hunter. Jacob, on the other hand, is more of a homebody, a tender of flocks and herds. Esau is the favorite of Isaac, their father; Rebekah, their mother, especially loves Jacob. We also learn how Esau sold his birthright as the older son to his brother, Jacob, for a bowl of stew. Esau was careless of the birthright; Jacob was a schemer, who took advantage of his brother to get it. Then when their father, Isaac, was on his deathbed, Rebekah and Jacob conspired together to get for Jacob the blessing of the first-born son, which Isaac intended for Esau.

It is because of that deception of his father that Jacob has been in exile for twenty years. He had to flee from Canaan because Esau threatened to kill him for stealing his blessing. Jacob fled to his mother's people in Paddan Aram and lived with his Uncle Laban.

During the years of his sojourn he had flourished. He had acquired two wives, two concubines, eleven sons, and great flocks and herds—even while engaging in a series of duplicitous episodes with Laban (wives, flocks and herds). He had grown wealthy—in his day, wealth was considered manifest evidence of God's blessing. When Jacob fled from Canaan, God had promised him a blessing in a dramatic dream of angels ascending and descending a stairway into heaven.

When some twenty years had passed, God told Jacob it was time for him to go home, to return to Canaan. His relationship with Laban had become strained because of Jacob's "success." It was time to go back to his people. In typical Jacob fashion, he leaves with all his family and property without saying a word to his uncle, Laban. When Laban learns about Jacob's leaving, he pursues him, but God warns Laban in a dream not to harm Jacob.

And so, delivered from the threat behind him, Jacob now faces the threat before him—his brother, Esau, whose last words about Jacob were a threat to kill him. And even as he turns to face this enemy, Jacob meets messengers sent by

God—presumably to encourage him and remind him of God's presence with him.

Jacob is concerned about Esau, but hoping that twenty years have mellowed him. He sends messengers to him with obsequious greetings, but the messengers return to say that Esau is coming to meet him with four hundred men. The only logical inference of bringing four hundred men is that Esau plans to attack him, so Jacob is afraid. He divides his company and his animals into two camps, thinking if Esau attacks one camp maybe the other can escape. Then, Jacob thinks to pray. He reminds God of the promises He has made to him and he prays for deliverance from Esau.

Now, praying was a good thing—isn't it always! But Jacob couldn't leave the matter in God's hands. He prayed, but then he kept worrying. So he took large numbers of animals from his flocks and herds and sent them ahead to Esau hoping to appease Esau's wrath with these gifts.

Finally, under cover of night, he took his family across the stream of the Jabbok, and he was left alone. And here, at this critical juncture in Jacob's life, we come to today's text. And what a strange and peculiar text it is. A mighty man sets upon Jacob in the night and wrestles with him until dawn. Neither man is able to subdue the other, and eventually, the man strikes Jacob a blow at his hip joint to weaken him.

Jacob is far from stupid. He figures out that this is no ordinary man he's contending with. And so, he asks for a blessing before he will release his hold on this divine being. In typical Jacob fashion, he wants to reap a benefit for himself. This was a smart move on Jacob's part, but what is this wrestling match all about? Is this God wrestling with one of his creatures? Really?

Why would God do such a thing? Is there something about Jacob that requires this sort of encounter for God to get Jacob's attention? To get God's message through to Jacob?

In response to Jacob's demand for a blessing, the "man" asks Jacob his name. If this is God wrestling with Jacob, clearly God knows Jacob's name, so why ask? The point is that in giving his name, Jacob was confessing his nature. He had to own up to who he was, the person he had been all his life. The name Jacob designated its owner as a crafty manipulator, a deceiver, one who was always scheming to improve his lot in life, often at the expense of someone else.

Now was the moment of truth for Jacob. In the words of Allen Ross, Professor of Old Testament and Hebrew at Beeson Divinity School, "Here the "heel-catcher" was crippled and had to identify his true nature before he could be blessed."

The blessing comes in Jacob's receiving a new name. This renaming of Jacob tells us that his assailant had the authority to impart a new name and new status. This action is the only clue to the assailant's identity, which he clearly considers unnecessary to impart ("Why do you ask my name?"). Jacob's new name is Israel, meaning "God contends," "God fights," a name that will be a reminder of this fight for Jacob and for all his descendants. His new name also results in a changed character.

No longer was Jacob to be a deceiver, one who sought his own advantage by conniving and cheating. Instead, as Israel, one who had fought with God and survived, he was to carry on the line of God's promises to his own and future generations.

Jacob becoming "Israel" marked the purifying of Jacob's character. God broke Jacob's physical strength and Jacob came finally to realize he was in the hands of One against whom it was useless to struggle. He emerged from this encounter with God a changed man, one worthy of the patriarchal role God had for him.

And in the immediate situation, the message for Jacob is clear: He had seen God face to face and been delivered. He could and must trust God's gracious and powerful provisions, not his own natural strength.

Having wrestled with God and survived, how could he fear Esau, a mere mortal? Now, with confidence, he could move forward to meet Esau without fear, not in his own paltry strength, but with the blessing and protection of God.

Are you, like me, prone to shake your head over Jacob and wonder why such a clever fellow as Jacob can't seem to get the message and trust God to fulfill his promises? God has protected him and blessed him at every turn—in spite of Jacob's devious ways.

Do you marvel that God would choose such a seemingly unlikely person to be the instrument of his blessing to all peoples? A cheat, a deceiver, a sly and crafty manipulator?

What's wrong with this picture?

When I stand outside the story, that's what I think. But when I get closer and project myself into the story, I come to realize, with startling clarity: I am Jacob; Jacob is me!

Not in the sense of being a cheat or a deceiver, BUT I too, am chosen of God in Jesus Christ. I am the recipient of God's great and precious promises. God has blessed my life and protected me, over and over again. Yet, how often do I beat the air, anxiously reaching out for every resource at hand to meet the threats and challenges of my life instead of trusting God's power and provision?

Of course, our culture encourages us to take care of ourselves. We are rugged individualists, applauded for employing our strength and energy to "succeed" in life's battles. After all, "Heaven helps those who help themselves"—right? Actually, that's a proverb from Aesop's fables, not from the Bible.

Do we, sometimes, in our supposed self-sufficiency, have to be "crippled" by God so he can bless us? Are we, like Jacob, inclined to forget God's protection and blessing in the past so that we face the present with fear instead of confident faith in our victorious God?

Do we need to be reminded that God has the power to overcome all our enemies—maybe not physical enemies such as Jacob faced, but the things that we fear and worry about—a fractured economy, inept national leaders, job insecurities, family crises—all sorts of enemies to our peace of mind and trust in God?

The message of this text for us is that God is able and God is willing—God wants to put his divine strength to work on our behalf—but we have to admit our own weakness, our own helplessness. We have to let God be in control and trust in his promises and provisions.

Do you, like me, need to offer a prayer of repentance for trying to go your own way, in your own strength instead of living like a believer—trusting in God to make your way through? Will you pray that prayer with me?

I frankly do not remember the occasion for which I prepared and preached this sermon. Perhaps a Wednesday night message?

One Necessary Thing
Luke 10:38-42

This text about Mary and Martha recounts a familiar event for most of us. I suspect most men tend to tune out a message preached on this passage. After all, it deals with women and household work. It's a woman thing.

But not so fast. While it is true that the situation focuses on two women, the truth expressed extends beyond them. It teaches a universal lesson for ALL believers.

Look closely at the text and perhaps we can fill in some gaps. Martha appears to be head of the household, and thus justifiably feels the responsibility of a host. Put yourself in her place. When you entertain a guest of Jesus' status you want everything to be perfect.

As the scene develops we see Mary at the feet of Jesus in the posture of a disciple. While it is true that Mary is taking on a role normally reserved for men, that is not the issue here. A natural question rises as to where are the disciples? Is this a situation that calls to mind Jesus' parable about the "ninety and nine"? The Twelve had already made their decision about Jesus, and he was always instructing and training them, but Martha needs some attention from the Master.

Martha wants to give her very best service to Jesus, and that is a good thing. The problem is that she has allowed this good intention to become a poisonous obsession.

Will Jesus go hungry if the meal is simple? Will Jesus be offended if the napkins aren't folded "just so"? Will harm be done if the table is not elaborately laid out? No, No, and No. Will Jesus think less of Martha if her hostessing isn't perfect? Martha may think so.

The issue is that Martha has turned this opportunity to serve Jesus into a stage for herself. She wants Jesus' attention and approval and tries to "earn" it by her works of service.

Mary wants something, too. She wants to be with Jesus. Not burdened with responsibility for the household, she pursues her own agenda: getting as close as possible to Jesus. It may well be that Martha wants that, too, which may be part of her resentment—not only that Mary isn't helping her, but Mary is getting what Martha also wants.

It is interesting to note that the heroine never speaks. Her example does. The conversation takes place between Martha and Jesus, but Mary is the focus of attention. However, Martha doesn't address Mary with her frustration. She seems to hold Jesus accountable for Mary's failure to help.

Is Martha's cry really finished at "Don't you care . . .?"

Don't you care about me, Jesus?

Do you care only for my sister?

Show me that you care for me! Notice all the effort I am putting forth for you! Don't I merit your attention?

Jesus' response is compassionate, caring, and warm, but he confronts Martha's issues. Can you hear the implications of his chiding:

"Martha, you've worked yourself into a state of resentment and anger. How does this kind of attitude serve and minister to me? Your peevishness undermines the value of your service. All of this "to-do" is only necessary in your mind. You are serving yourself more than serving me. What matters is that we spend time together. Mary has understood the most important thing, the one necessary thing—spending time with me, learning of me, befriending me with her presence."

I remember an occasion when a friend of mine attended the wedding of a young man with whom she had gone through some specialized training. As she delivered her wedding gift to him, he accepted it graciously, but said, "Your presence is gift enough." My own spirit has often echoed that sentiment when spending time with a cherished friend. It seems likely that is what Jesus wanted in the home of these friends. As he faced the coming suffering of his trial and crucifixion, he desired the comfort and companionship of his dearest friends.

In Jesus' commendation of Mary, I hear echoes of Deuteronomy 8:3, a text that Jesus himself used in combating the temptations of Satan: "One does not live by bread alone, but by every word that comes from the mouth of the Lord."

Here I think is the root of this text's application for us today, men as well as women. Our diet is deficient. Too often we are trying to live by bread alone. As a result, we exist in survival mode, not the healthy, wholesome, flourishing mode God intends and wants to provide for us.

Too often we choose Martha's part—working for the Lord, so we think, but our service has become self-oriented, trying to get God's notice, wanting God's commendation, when all we need to do to get God's attention is to seek his presence.

Now don't hear me saying that service or work is bad—far from it. God has created us for "good works," as Paul tells us plainly in Ephesians 2:10. But the works are the result, the overflow, of being with Christ, not a substitute for it. Works do not nourish relationships; relationships are nourished by spending time together. It may be time spent in shared work, but work alone doesn't build relationship. Martha's work was not unimportant, but it was joyless. It was burdensome and worrying, causing problems in her relationships.

Jesus calls us to relationship first, and then sends us to serve. Remember Mark 3:14? Jesus chose twelve that they might be with him and then he would send them out to preach. And the result of serving out of relationship is described in Acts 4:13. When Peter and John were arrested while preaching in the Temple courtyard, the people were amazed by their ministry and "recognized that these men had been with Jesus."

So the question I would leave us with is this: Do our lives and ministries testify that we have been with Jesus? Or are we serving out of habit, or obligation, or desire for human approval?

Martha and Mary both had important roles to play, but Jesus is clear that the one necessary thing for both of them and for all of us is spending time in his presence.

Don't try to live by bread alone. Feast on the One who is the true and living bread!

Occasionally my pastor asks me to fill in for him on a Sunday morning or Wednesday night when he is away. This message I prepared on such an occasion for a Wednesday night gathering shortly after Easter.

Resurrection Power
Vestavia Hills Baptist Church
Wednesday, May 20, 2015

I have been thinking this year, more than in previous years, about Eastertide, the fifty days between Easter Sunday and Pentecost. Not just celebrating on Easter Sunday, but reflecting on the lingering impact of the Easter event, what I'm calling resurrection power.

We heard about it Sunday morning in the text of Ephesians 1, Paul's prayer for the Ephesian Christians. He prays that they may know "the immeasurable greatness of his power toward us who believe, according to the working of his great might that he worked in Christ when he raised him from the dead and seated him at his right hand in the heavenly places" (vv. 19-20).

I like the way Jean Sophia Pigott expressed this idea in lines from a hymn she wrote:

Make my life a bright outshining
Of Thy life, that all may see
Thine own resurrection power
Mightily put forth in me;

The reason, I think, that I've not given this more thought in the past is tied to my long tradition in Baptist life. Many of you, like me, are lifetime Baptists, and Baptists focus on the cross, the Good Friday event of Easter weekend. I grew up seeing crosses on church steeples, singing hymns about the cross, and internalizing the gospel message of the cross.

And I am not disparaging the cross. I'm very grateful for my evangelical roots in the Baptist faith tradition, and truly, without Good Friday there would be no Easter Sunday. Without Christ's death, there would be no resurrection. So I ardently affirm the cross and all it stands for.

What I have realized, however, in thinking about Eastertide, is that I have been prone to underemphasize Christ's resurrection. Oh, I joyfully enter into the glorious celebration of Easter Sunday morning, but then, what? Easter Monday dawns and what do I carry forward into my life from that resurrection high point? Well, I certainly see Christ's resurrection as a forerunner to my own. I cling firmly to the expectation that one day, after my death, I, too, will experience resurrection. That I will be changed—transformed—into a new being in the presence of God forever.

Again, I don't want to discount that belief. The thing that troubles me, though, is that this belief, as I have received and hold to it, seems to relegate the significance of Easter Sunday and resurrection to my life after I die. I suspect the same is true for many of you.

As I've pondered this whole idea of the lingering presence of Easter beyond that culminating Sunday celebration, I've come to embrace some new understandings. I think I knew these things in the recesses of my mind, but have never really given them the attention they deserve.

So, I want to share with you some of the insights I've gained from thinking more intentionally about the resurrection, "Living the Resurrection," as Eugene Peterson, veteran pastor and theologian, titles his book on the subject.

When I was teaching New Testament, one of the visuals I used with my students was to draw a horizontal time line extending from creation to eternity. At the beginning, I put creation and at the opposite end, I put eternity. In between, I drew an arrow downward to signify Christ coming to earth from heaven. To the right of that to signify some thirty years, I drew a cross, representing Christ's crucifixion. To the right of that, I put an upward arrow to indicate the resurrection and ascension. Then, I put brackets around a section at the eternity end of the line and drew a dotted line from it to the present. This represented a chunk of the future that had come into the present with the resurrection of Jesus and the coming of the Holy Spirit.

N. T. Wright expresses the idea this way:

"Jesus's resurrection is the beginning of God's new project not to snatch people away from earth to heaven but to colonize earth with the life of heaven. That, after all, is what the Lord's Prayer is about." (*Surprised by Hope: Rethinking Heaven, the Resurrection, and the Mission of the Church*)

I think that is an accurate representation of what Christ's resurrection means for Christians. After Christ's resurrection and ascension to heaven, God's Holy Spirit was poured out upon all believers. We know that part of our theology, but do we realize it in our daily living. For the most part, I'm inclined to say "No."

Christ's resurrection means much more for us than just the assurance of our resurrection after death. Among many other things, it confirms God's promises and God's power. We read in our Bibles that God delivered the Hebrews from Egypt, parted the Red Sea for them to pass through, fed them forty years in the wilderness, enabled them to conquer the inhabitants of the Promised Land, and we say, "That's all history."

We read in the New Testament about Jesus performing all sorts of miracles—causing the blind to see, the lame to walk, the deaf to hear. We even learn that Jesus raised people from the dead—the Roman official's little daughter, the widow of Nain's son, and Lazarus, and we say that was a unique time in salvation history.

Why do we do that? Why do we restrict God's amazing supernatural power to biblical times? Where do we have any basis for thinking that God has withdrawn that power from us? Among Christ's final instructions to his followers is the text in Matthew 28:19-20, which we refer to as "The Great Commission":

"Therefore go and make disciples of all nations, baptizing them in the name of the Father and of the Son and of the Holy Spirit, and teaching them to obey everything I have commanded you. And surely I am with you always, to the very end of the age."

Do you remember what Jesus said immediately before that in verse 18? "All authority in heaven and on earth has been given to me. Therefore, Go, make disciples, and teach. And, I am with you until the end of the age." It sounds to me like Jesus is saying his power is with us forever.

In fact, we occasionally read or hear stories of seemingly miraculous things that happen in our world today and we shake our heads in awe and wonder, but we really don't expect miraculous things to happen. We pray for miracles, but all too often, we pray without expectation. Yet, we've seen miraculous things happen right here in our congregation. Think about just a few among us who have been delivered from seemingly unrecoverable illnesses. Clearly, God doesn't always spare his saints when they are physically afflicted, but sometimes, for his own reasons, he does.

The point is, God has the power to overcome anything and everything that life throws at us, and because of Christ's resurrection, we have access to God's power. As Paul says in Ephesians 3:10: "I want to know Christ and the power of his resurrection."

And God's miracles aren't just about physical healing. Let me share with you some events I consider miraculous in my own life. Back in 1988, I was working as an Associate Director of Birmingham Public Library. I'd worked hard to get where I was and believed the Lord had made those things possible, but after I'd thoroughly learned the job and settled in, I developed an uneasy sense that maybe my life was too comfortable.

I began to ask myself and God if that was all there was, if his plan for me was just to coast through the remainder of my working years enjoying the benefits of my position. After some two years of praying and thinking about all this, one day in a flash, I sensed God calling me to a new vocation—one of teaching the Bible. I realized that would require a seminary education, but would you believe this calling occurred only two months after Samford University announced they would be opening a Divinity School that fall? The timing of that event seemed to me a divine congruence of calling and provision.

I was taking a few days off from work when I experienced that call. The following Monday, when I went back to work and walked into the Director's office, his first words to me after a greeting were, "Have you ever thought about going to seminary?"

I probably don't need to tell you that by that time, I had no question but that God was doing a work in and for me. My boss and I sat together for two hours that morning talking about what I had experienced and how we might practically enable me to keep working and enroll in Beeson Divinity

School that fall. I don't have time to tell you all the details, but God used my boss as just one of His partners in the work God was doing to accomplish God's will in my life.

Later that summer, I got a phone call from a long-time family friend, a faithful believer, who asked if we could meet for lunch. After a nice meal together, he said, "Two years ago I felt the Lord urging me to put aside some money for you. I didn't know why, but I put $10,000 in a CD for you, and did the same thing last year. Recently I've felt the Lord telling me the time has come to give that money to you." With those words he handed me a check for $21,600! It was my delight to reveal to him what God intended with his gift.

Those are only two examples of the many ways God made provision for me to follow his calling in my life. There are many, many more. So, you see, I have personal reasons to believe that God's power is still available to us even in our world today. But in order for that power to be manifested to me, I had to trust God's promise that he would be with me always and to believe that he really does have all power in heaven and on earth.

I won't claim it was an easy thing to do—to give up my comfortable career, sell my house, move to Texas, and earn a Ph.D. Even with all God had done for me, I still wondered how I could pull off my part of it. I'd read about everything required to earn a Ph.D. and thought, "How can I do all this?" But then, the Lord delivered the ultimate conviction. One day when I was mulling all these things in my mind, the thought came to me: "If God can part the seas to accomplish his purposes and raise people from the dead, how can I doubt his power to do what He wills in my life?"

The next several years were both the scariest and most exhilarating time of my Christian pilgrimage. As worldly concerns would assail me, I would be scared; as I remembered God's provision, I would be elated. Those two emotions danced in tandem within my spirit, but God's attention to every detail and his provisions for me were so powerful, I couldn't resist. I didn't want to resist.

What I am trying to illustrate and emphasize here is resurrection power. Jesus commissioned his disciples (and us) to go into the world trusting in his authority and power over all things in heaven and on earth. Why are we so often, like the disciples, "of little faith"?

I know that some of you here, probably more than I know, feel you are facing great giants in your lives. Circumstances, relationships, health concerns, and maybe other burdens are staring you down. It's natural to feel overwhelmed, to wonder how you're going to make it through this next phase of your journey. I understand how scary that can be. But I want to testify that our God is able. Able to deliver us, if it's in His will, or able to sustain us through the valley of the shadows, if that's His will.

I don't mean to diminish the harsh realities you may be facing, but I do want to encourage you, even urge you, to offer up your burden to the One who has all power. The One who holds authority over all people and all situations. I can't promise you that God will make your difficulties disappear, but I can testify that God has promised never to leave you and that He is "able to do immeasurably more than all we can ask or imagine, according to his power that is at work within us." (Ephesians 3:20-21)

So, I encourage you not to be timid about going forward with your lives, but boldly step forth filled with all the hope and joy that Easter brings. After all, we are Easter people. We serve the One who has all power in heaven and on earth. We can join with the Apostle Paul in saying, "I want to know Christ and the power of his resurrection."

Meditations

God has blessed me throughout my life with wonderful friends who have been the presence of God to me. One of those friends was Lester Barker, who served as Minister of Music in several Birmingham area churches. When he died in March 2010, his adult children asked me to deliver the homily at his funeral. In addition to the personal reminiscences I recounted, I composed the following tribute based on the Proverbs 31 tribute to a godly woman.

Paraphrase on Proverbs 31

Who can find a man of noble character?
For he is worth more than gold or silver.
His wife has full confidence in him and she lacks nothing of value.
He brings her good, not harm, all the days of his life.
He engages in honorable labor and works with an eager heart.
He is among the princes of men, delighting in serving his God.
He gets up early to earn food for his table and shelter for his family.
He makes sound judgments and teaches his children to fear God.
He works vigorously and glories in the strength God gives him.
He sees that his ministry is pleasing and he works at it day and night.
He stretches out his hand to the outcast and extends his care to the needy.
He does not fear for his life or his family, for they are protected by God.
He serves God faithfully and gives his children a goodly heritage.
His wife is virtuous and her deeds admired by all.
He gives of himself in service to others and genuinely cares for them.
He is clothed with strength and dignity; he faces the future confidently.
He speaks with wisdom, and faithful instruction is on his tongue.
He watches over the affairs of his household and diligently tends them.
His children rise up and call him blessed; his wife also, and she praises him, saying:
"Many men are virtuous and honorable, but you surpass them all."
Charm is deceitful and looks are fleeting, but a man who fears the Lord will be honored.
Give him credit for what he has accomplished, and let his works declare his praise.

Quite a few of my former students have become my dear friends, and I have been privileged to participate in significant events in their lives and ministries. One of the greatest honors, for me, is being invited to participate in their ordination services. The message below I prepared and delivered for such a service.

Spiritual Formation Charge
Matthew 6:5-8; Mark 1:35-38
Ordination Service for Cary Hughes
Saturday, 29 January 2011

Cary, you have studied long and hard and learned a lot, including the meaning of spiritual formation: becoming more and more like Jesus by cooperating with the Holy Spirit's work within you. You have committed yourself to spiritual formation because . . .

It is God's will for you—so you can better serve him and so you can be a better shepherd of his people.

Many pastors know this, but the demands of ministry are such that you are always in danger of allowing spiritual formation to become secondary in importance and thus neglected. But your spiritual nurture must remain primary for you, just as it was for Jesus.

You have asked me to focus my remarks on the two Scripture texts: Matthew 6:5-8 and Mark 1:35-38. These two passages are particularly apt because they deal with the disciple's life of prayer.

Here are truths for the spiritual formation of prayer that these texts reveal, first from the Matthew passage:

Notice how Jesus begins this instruction: "When" you pray. Jesus took it for granted that prayer would be a part of his followers' lives.

Next is the "how" of praying: Do it away from spectators. Prayer is a private encounter between you and God. Others should know of it not because you do it where they can see you praying, but because they see its result in the quality of your life and ministry.

Minimize your words. Your eloquence is immaterial. Prayer is more about your listening and God's speaking. God already knows your heart; He already knows what you need. What he desires from you is that you open your heart to him with honesty and humility. Pray simply and trust the Holy Spirit to interpret your thoughts and feelings.

Now, from Mark:

In the opening of this passage, in verse 35, we see a picture of Jesus' own prayer life. What better example could you hope to follow?

We read that Jesus got up "Very early in the morning" and went out to pray. He was intentional about his prayer time. It was so early that it was "still dark." That way he could ensure he would be unseen by others. He knew this was a private affair between himself and his Father. You will need to schedule this prayer time early in your day so that it doesn't get crowded out by the demands of your day.

Additionally, Jesus "left the house." He separated himself from even those closest and dearest to him for this private, intimate encounter. And he chose a "solitary place." He planned and chose to be uninterrupted in this special time reserved for just himself and God. You must plan and choose to be uninterrupted in this time reserved for just God and you.

When Peter and the others found Jesus, their concern was "Everyone is looking for you." One of the greatest temptations of ministry is the temptation to follow the crowd, to go where the demand seems loudest and greatest. You must reject this voice. All the ministry was not completed when Jesus withdrew for his time of prayer. You must not allow the ministry demands of those around you to control the use of your time.

Jesus' response to his disciples was, "Let's go to other villages . . . that is why I have come." He stayed true to the mission God had given him and didn't allow the expectations of others to divert him from it. The time he spent in his solitary place of prayer enabled him to refocus, to remember his mission, and to recommit to his purpose. It gave him strength to resist the call of the crowd and wisdom to remain true to his divine assignment.

Sometimes your mission may be to the multitudes; sometimes to one small place and group. Neither assignment is greater than the other. What matters is what God has called you to do.

Be faithful WHEREVER God sends you. The courage and commitment to serve wherever is gained in the solitary place of prayer. Where you minister should be immaterial to you—only that it is where God leads.

In summary, here are instructions from Scripture for your prayer life:

→Make prayer habitual, but not routine.
→Make prayer private, an encounter between you and God alone.

→Make prayer intentional—schedule it.
→Use prayer as listening time to keep your purpose the same as God's purpose for you.
→Remember prayer is the source of your strength and enablement for abiding in Christ.

Among the dear saints in my home church are a retired missionary couple, Bob and Mavis Hardy. Even though their service in Japan was completed many years ago, they continue to be involved in missions activities locally. For several years, Mavis served as Coordinator for our local Baptist Association's International Day of Prayer for World Missions. For two of those years, she invited me to deliver the message for that annual event. I prepared and delivered this sermon for one of those occasions.

By My Spirit
Zechariah 4:1-10
Vestavia Hills Baptist Church
International Day of Prayer for World Missions
6 November 2011

The theme for this year's World Missions emphasis, "In Step with the Spirit," reminded me of a favorite text in the book of Zechariah. Those who compiled our Bible categorize Zechariah as a minor prophet, and as such, his book doesn't get much attention. However, he is minor only in that his writing is short. His message, nevertheless, reveals important truths from God.

Let me refresh your memory about Zechariah. He was a priest who lived in post-exilic times. He returned to Jerusalem from Babylonian captivity around 520 A.D. This was a difficult time in the life of the Hebrew people. Those who had returned from exile had made a beginning of re-establishing their life in and around Jerusalem. They had rebuilt the altar and the foundation of the destroyed temple, but the local people opposed them, and in time, they became discouraged and quit building. They felt overwhelmed with the difficulty of the task. It seemed so great and their efforts seemed so feeble.

At this point, Zechariah enters the scene. He received a series of visions with messages from God, and today I want to focus on the fifth vision, recorded in Zechariah 4:1-10. In this particular vision, Zechariah saw a sort of multi-wick lamp stand with an endless supply of oil from two olive trees on either side of it. The angel who attends this vision reveals that the two olive trees are symbolic of God's Spirit.

Two points in particular I want to make based on this text. First, in verse six, we hear the angel deliver words from the Lord: "Not by might, nor by power, but by my Spirit." These words remind us that it is God's Spirit who accomplishes God's purposes. We often see our work for God falter and we try to exert more effort, thinking we're not doing enough. But God's response teaches us to seek His Spirit and trust Him to accomplish his will.

The second point derives from verse ten: "Whoever despised the day of small things shall rejoice." Here is God's promise that even things that seem small in our eyes can be used of God. In Zechariah's day, the temple being rebuilt was small and ordinary in comparison with the grandeur and beauty of the temple that had been destroyed. Yet, God would use it to begin the restoration of the people of Israel to their land.

We, too, can easily feel overwhelmed by the size of our task, the immensity of the need we see all around. We consider our efforts to be feeble and ineffective. Perhaps we feel that way about our prayers. How often do we hear the expression: "All I can do is pray for you"? And it is said apologetically, as if it is something small and insignificant. Maybe we've said it that way ourselves. But God told Zechariah to challenge the people who despised the day of small things. God told him the tasks God had given the people would be accomplished, not by military might or any sort of human strength, but by the power of God's Spirit.

We, too, need to remember that God empowers and uses our efforts through His Spirit, which is limitless. Remember God's words to Paul "my strength is made perfect in weakness" (2 Cor. 12:9), and Jesus' words about the mustard seed: "It is the smallest of all seeds, but when it has grown, it is larger than all the garden plants and becomes a tree" (Matt. 13:31).

So, I offer two truths from God's Word to encourage us today as we face an overwhelming world of need:

1) God is at work in our efforts, and by His Spirit, his purposes will be accomplished.

2) We must not be discouraged if our efforts seem small, because God uses the small and the weak and magnifies what we do into the great work of His kingdom.

If we stay in step with God's Spirit, we can persevere and find fulfillment even in the seemingly small tasks we do, for God measures our effort by a different scale.

A quote from Brother Lawrence seems a good way to summarize this message. In his little book, *The Practice of the Presence of God*, the compiler records this saying: "It is not the size of the task that matters to God, but the love with which it is done."

So, be faithful to your work for God. Remember that prayer is not a small part of that work, and trust God's Spirit to work out God's purposes.

Devotions

Several years ago I sat in on a seminary class, The Writing Minister, *taught by Denise George. Over the course of the semester, she assigned us a variety of types of Christian writing. One of those assignments was to compose a devotion of the sort we might encounter in* The Upper Room *or* Open Windows. *This devotion was one of my attempts.*

The Better Thing
Luke 10: 38-42

I have heard many sermons based on this incident at the home of Martha and Mary in the life of Jesus, and I confess I always identify with Mary. I much prefer my books to cooking and cleaning, so maybe my claim to be a Mary is self-serving. Actually, I think all of us have characteristics of both Martha and Mary within us, but one or the other tends to dominate. Still, I have often taken satisfaction, if not pride, in feeling more attachment to Mary's role.

I was brought up short this morning by observing that I had taken on Martha's role. I wasn't preparing a meal for anyone. I was performing my usual morning exercise routine, a time when I normally close my eyes and focus inward, taking the opportunity to offer prayers of intercession for family and friends. However, this morning, I couldn't focus. I would begin speaking to God, but soon I found that I was mentally elsewhere—planning my route through Walmart when I went to buy groceries later in the morning. I pulled my thoughts back to my prayers and started again, but soon found myself thinking about tomorrow's plans for meeting a friend I hadn't seen in a long time.

As I once again pulled my thoughts back to my prayers, I thought of Jesus' words to Martha in today's Scripture: "You are worried and distracted by many things; there is need of only one thing. Mary has chosen the better part." I, like Martha, was allowing myself to be distracted from the better thing, indeed, the best thing—time with Jesus. Lent is a time for repentance and reflection, both of which I obviously needed at the beginning of this day. Interestingly, as soon as I confessed my distractedness to God in prayer, my unsettled mind became focused and I was able to carry out my prayer time without further distractions.

Are you, too, finding yourself distracted from the better thing, spending time with Jesus? Confess it, repent of it, and tune in to what our Lord would say to you today.

I wrote my Ph.D. dissertation on Jesus' encounter with a Samaritan woman recorded in John's Gospel. As a result, I am invited, from time to time, to speak on some aspect of that biblical text. I don't recall the specific invitation to which this item refers, but this was another attempt to compose a devotion in the style of The Upper Room/Open Windows *daily devotion magazines.*

Christian Hospitality
John 4:4-26

Recently I was asked to teach a study on Christian hospitality based on Jesus' encounter with the Samaritan woman in John 4. I had never thought of that biblical story in terms of hospitality, but the idea intrigued me.

The word "hospitality" literally means "kindness to strangers." Since Jesus was the stranger traveling through Samaria, it would seem the Samaritan woman should be offering hospitality to Jesus, but the biblical story says that Jesus initiated their conversation. She responded with surprise because Jews had nothing to do with Samaritans, and men didn't speak to women in public. So how was it that this story revealed Christian hospitality?

I identified four aspects of hospitality illustrated by this story: availability, approachability, adaptability, and acceptability. Jesus made himself available to the Samaritan woman when he chose to travel through her land. He showed himself approachable by engaging her in conversation. He demonstrated adaptability by accommodating to her limited understanding and finding a way to reveal the truth to her. Finally, Jesus provided acceptability to the Samaritan woman by telling her how to please God.

Taking this story as a model of Christian hospitality, I, too, can share God's love with people I encounter. I can slow down enough to be available to people. I can initiate conversations with strangers, thereby demonstrating approachability. I can be adaptable to another's circumstances, and I can accept people where they are and point them to God. How better to demonstrate Christian hospitality than imitating Jesus?

The devotion style of writing that Denise George taught us necessarily limited us to a text of 300-350 words, a limitation imposed by publishers of these devotional books because it allowed them to print each day's entry on a single page. It is, at least theoretically, one of the simplest forms of composition. I wrote this devotion for her class.

God's Faithfulness
Psalm 37:23-28

I was young and now I am old, but I have never seen the righteous forsaken.

--Psalm 37:25 (NRSV)

My 87-year-old Uncle Francis is experiencing many challenges of aging. His eyesight is failing and an uncontrollable tremor in his right hand makes actions such as bathing, shaving, and writing extremely difficult. Ministrokes are slowly robbing him of his memory and mental abilities. As a young man, Uncle Francis was independent and self-reliant, so one of the most painful effects of these physical changes for him is the need to depend on others for help.

Recently, his increasing frailty made it obvious that he could no longer live alone and must move to an assisted-living home. When my brother and I told him of these plans, he began to name the people he would miss: the managers of the restaurant around the corner who prepare his meals every day and never accept payment; his former co-workers who come every year at Christmas and his birthday bringing him gifts; his former Sunday School teacher who always shows up in times of crisis.

As he spoke of these kindnesses, I was reminded of today's Scripture text. Uncle Francis had served God faithfully while he was young and able, and God proved faithful to him then. Now, by using the people around Uncle Francis to care for him, God keeps his promise of not forsaking this righteous one when he is old. What a comfort to be reminded that God will never leave us nor forsake us. What a blessing to be an instrument of God's care in the life of elders we know.

I was quite interested when, a few years ago, some letters written by Mother Teresa to her spiritual director were published revealing the spiritual struggles she endured across the years of her magnificent ministry to the poor in Calcutta. I was inspired to write this devotion after reading that book.

Where Is Your God?
Psalm 42

My tears have been my food day and night, while people say to me continually, "Where is your God?"

-Psalm 42:3

Publication, in recent years, of a book of letters written by Mother Teresa during her more than forty years of service among the poorest of the poor in Calcutta reveals that she was often plagued by doubts about God. These letters have aroused worldwide attention because they reveal a tumultuous inner spiritual life seemingly inconsistent with the settled faith and assurance of the public persona of the "Saint of Calcutta."

This disturbance of her popular image has led to questions of Mother Teresa's suitability for sainthood. Should one whose faith wavers and retreats legitimately be categorized as an exemplary Christian, a saint? Spokespersons from within the Catholic faith answer confidently and insistently, "yes."

Release of the letters is not an attempt by some anti-religious reporter to defame or discredit the nun. Rather, Brian Kolodiejchuk, M.C., Director of the Mother Teresa Center, and the one charged with making the case for her sainthood, made the letters available. Written as private communications between Mother Teresa and her spiritual advisors, the letters were never intended to become public, but Kolodiejchuk has published them because he believes they give proof of "her most spiritually heroic act"—her perseverance in missions despite her sense of spiritual dryness.

In truth, periods of spiritual darkness are not unknown among Catholic saints, and St. John of the Cross, the 16th-century Spanish mystic, gave us language for such times—the dark night of the soul. Still, Mother Teresa's may be the most extreme case ever recorded because it lasted so long.

Disparagers of Christianity and detractors of Mother Teresa have seized upon the letters as additional evidence of their claims. While the thread of feeling separated from God forms a consistent pattern in the letters, the dominant theme is unwavering devotion to God:

"As for me, I have nothing—since I have not got Him . . . How terrible it is to be without God—no prayer—no faith—no love. —The only thing that still remains—is the conviction that the work is His. . .. And I cling to this . . . in spite of all these—I want to be faithful to Him—to spend myself for Him, to love Him not for what He gives but for what He takes—to be at His disposal. —I do not ask Him to change His attitude towards me or His plans for me. —I ask Him to use me . . ."

And use her, God did . . . and does. Can you think of a more meaningful way of life? I can't. Would God but give me a measure of her courage and faithfulness!

Lectures

I wrote my Ph.D. dissertation on John 4, the account of Jesus' encounter with a Samaritan woman at Jacob's well. My personal contribution to the study of this text is an interpretation of this woman that provides an alternative to the traditional treatment of her in church history, in art, and in literature. Whenever and wherever I have shared my interpretation, people have approached me afterward to know if it is available in print. It is available as the final chapter of my dissertation, which was published by E.J. Brill in 2002, and I include it here for those who want to have it.

Who Was the Samaritan Woman?
John 4:1-42

The story of Jesus and the Samaritan woman, the so-called "woman at the well," recorded in Chapter 4 of John's Gospel is a favorite of most Bible readers and hearers. What is the key to its popularity? I think at least part of what draws us to it is the unique individual with whom Jesus converses there.

New Testament scholars have traditionally focused their study of this passage on Jesus' revelation of his identity as the Messiah to this non-Jewish woman. In contrast to his repeated instructions to the Jews he healed, not to reveal his identity, he forthrightly declares his divine identity to her.

Another approach scholars take is to reflect upon Jesus' statements about God and worship, that God seeks worshipers who will worship him in spirit and truth, not those who practice empty rituals. And yet, I find this enigmatic Samaritan woman, with whom Christ converses, equally as interesting as the theology the text reveals.

Scholars haven't ignored the Samaritan woman herself, but the attention they have paid to her has generally been less than complimentary. Some regard her as having no particular personality at all. They simply see her as a representative figure for the entire Samaritan people who had an incomplete knowledge of God. Others, homing in on verses 17-18, where Jesus reveals that she has had five husbands and is currently living with a man not her husband, conclude that she must be promiscuous, immoral, and probably adulterous. I choose to look at what the biblical text says and doesn't say about this woman, and offer an alternative interpretation.

When Jesus encountered the Samaritan woman, he had been in Jerusalem for the Jewish Passover where many people believed in him because of the "miraculous signs" he was performing. Shortly thereafter, Jesus departed for Galilee with his disciples, and it is this journey that provides the occasion for Jesus' encounter with the Samaritan woman.

First, it is interesting to consider why Jesus is here. Granted he is en route to Galilee, and travel through Samaria is the most direct route, but John uses a special Greek word, *edei*, which is translated "had to," or "it was necessary." In other places where John uses this particular verb, he uses it to describe something necessary to fulfill the will of God, some sort of divine compulsion. Was this meeting between Jesus and the Samaritan woman a "divine providential appointment?"

Consider, too, why Jesus was left alone at the well. Nowhere else in John's Gospel, other than at Jesus' arrest, do all the disciples go away and leave Jesus by himself. John reports the cause as Jesus being tired from the journey. Were the disciples not also tired? We do not know. The text leaves gaps we are left to fill with our own imagination. One possibility that occurs to me is God arranged it to be so.

You probably remember the story. Jesus stops to rest beside Jacob's well while his disciples go into the town in search of food. While he is resting, a Samaritan woman comes to the well for water, and Jesus asks her for a drink. She is astonished that he, a Jew, would even speak to her, a Samaritan, because of the intense hatred between those two peoples. In the conversation that ensues, Jesus uses the metaphor of water to lead her to believe in him. Then, as a result of her testimony, the whole populace of the town comes to seek Jesus.

In assessing the characterization of the Samaritan woman, there are essentially three defining moments in her conversation with Jesus. Our first impression of the woman comes in her initial response to Jesus' request for a drink. Our second leap of understanding comes in the part of the discourse when Jesus tells her to go get her husband and return. The third revealing moment occurs in her witness to the townspeople. How we interpret these three defining moments colors what our final impression of the woman will be, and it is important to note that multiple interpretations are possible. The words spoken by the woman and Jesus are a given, but we have some freedom for putting tone and inflection into those words and imagining the accompanying body language.

Jesus initiates the conversation with the woman, and her response to his request begins the intrigue for the reader in deciphering who she is (4:7-9). The narrator does not tell us that the woman is surprised or shocked by Jesus' request, but her words leave no doubt about her incredulity. Jesus has disrupted her world of expectation on two counts; he has violated both racial and gender taboos.

First, and most obviously, she is Samaritan and he is Jew. We know from historical sources about the hatred between Jews and Samaritans. Scholars debate the origins of the schism between them, but at the time of Jesus the animosity was predominantly religious. The Samaritans claimed common religious origins with the Jews, but their Scriptures were limited to the five books of Moses, Genesis through Deuteronomy. Furthermore, they worshiped on Mount Gerizim rather than in Jerusalem. The Jews considered the Samaritans ritually unclean and did not willingly have any association with them.

The second issue contributing to the woman's shock is that Jesus, a man, initiates speaking to her, a woman. Jesus was violating a Jewish cultural taboo that Jewish men were admonished to spend no time in conversation with a woman, especially not in public. Thus, the woman had double cause for her astonishment; Jesus was crossing the boundary between Jew and Samaritan and between woman and man.

The tone the reader projects onto the woman's response to Jesus' request for a drink will color significantly the reader's idea of the woman's character. Does she reply in an insulting, jeering manner, as if to throw in Jesus' face the fact that the Jews considered Samaritans irreligious, but would still ask a drink from one? That is certainly one possibility for understanding her attitude, but not the only one. I read here only shock and incredulity.

No doubt the woman had noticed Jesus sitting at the well as she approached. Possibly she had already perceived that he was a Jew, perhaps by his clothing. She had no expectation that he would even acknowledge her presence, much less speak to her. It is plausible to think that her response was not defensive or mocking, but simply surprise.

One reason for not attributing to her a hostile response is the very cultural circumstance that caused her to be shocked by Jesus' request. As a woman, a person of extremely little value or respect in the cultural milieu of first-century Palestine, she would not have had the audacity to make a saucy reply. Given that women were scarcely ever spoken to by men in public, it seems unlikely that when one was, she would respond in any unseemly way.

Another indication of the woman's sincerity is that in her next two responses, she addresses Jesus as *kurios*, used in the common sense of "sir." It is a respectful form of address, one that would not be compatible with a disdainful attitude and tone. Consequently, I do not find her words to Jesus scornful.

Here we have one of those narrative occurrences where we can't evaluate the intent of discourse by observing gestures and facial expressions or hearing vocal intonation. As readers we have to infer meaning. And I would argue that an inference of respect can just as readily be deduced from the text as its opposite, disrespect.

As Jesus keeps trying to lead the woman into a spiritual understanding of the living water, the woman's continuing insistence on keeping the conversation at a literal level may reflect some degree of intellectual dullness. Her life was very earth-bound, concerned with daily survival, and the conceptual level on which Jesus was conversing with her would likely have been an unaccustomed event. After all, she was trying to deal with her amazement that the conversation was even taking place, while trying to maintain some semblance of engagement with the ongoing discussion. It seems obvious that her cultural and educational circumstances did not provide her opportunity for this type of conversation. She may have been doing well just to maintain a literal understanding of what Jesus was saying.

With Jesus' next words to the woman, the narrative enters the second defining moment for understanding who she is. Realizing the need to take a different approach in order to break through her dogged literalism, Jesus abruptly redirects the conversation. He tells the woman to go, call her husband and come back (4:16). The woman, however, responds by telling him that she has no husband. Jesus acknowledges the truthfulness of her answer and then reveals his supernatural knowledge of her life story. Indeed, she does not have a husband, but she has over the course of her life been married to five husbands, and is now living with a man to whom she is not married (4:17-18).

Jesus' revelation of the woman's past has been the crux for traditional interpretation in establishing the kind of person this woman was. Hearing Jesus reveal her unusual marital history and her current apparently immoral living arrangement, most commentators conclude that the woman is promiscuous, perhaps even a prostitute.

This response seems logical on the surface because to have had five marriages elicits a judgmental reaction, at least from most contemporary readers. Such a marital history seems to imply that the person has little sense of commitment and has abandoned relationships readily. Such a person defies our Christian idea of marriage as a covenant relationship. Add to five marriages, the fact that the woman was now living with a man without the benefit of marriage and the reader's opinion of her is dramatically moved in a negative direction. Judgment of her immorality tends to be without consideration that an explanation might be found that does not condemn her.

However, I suggest that even here, at the point in the characterization of the woman where she is most vulnerable to judgment and condemnation, there is another possible interpretation. Based on our knowledge of the social and cultural values of first-century Palestine, why would it be unnatural to surmise that the woman is deserving of our sympathy rather than our opprobrium? Is it not possible that the woman had been married so many times because of economic and social reasons, rather than for lustful reasons? By what means, in her culture, could she survive by working for wages? In a society that granted to women essentially no social or legal standing apart from a responsible man—father, husband, brother or son--she can legitimately be considered a marginalized figure, subject to economic, social, and legal exploitation.

Women's rights were severely limited in first-century Palestinian culture. A woman had very little control over her own life, with both marriage and divorce being the prerogative of men. Her status in community life was more akin to that of slaves and children than to a responsible adult.

This woman, as all women of her day, was considered to be of limited importance. The biblical text tells us nothing about any children she might have had, but even if she did have sons, their responsibility for her would have been to try and arrange another marriage when a previous one ended in death or divorce.

It is important to note here that we do not know whether the woman's five husbands had died or had divorced her, but divorce was exclusively the husband's right. For this reason, the woman may well have either outlived her husbands, or at least some of them, or had been divorced by them, for perhaps no particular fault of her own, such as the inability to bear children. Since Jewish thought allowed a maximum of three marriages for a woman, the fact that she had been married five times indicates that her life had been especially difficult, and probably meant that she was an object of either pity or ridicule, or both.

The fact that she was now living with a man who was not her husband may not be a matter of her choice, but a matter of necessity in order to have the protection of a man and a place to live. If, having had five marriages, she is advanced in age and without means to support herself, having a man to provide for her may have been her only means of survival in a cultural system that made no provision for the independent maintenance of a woman alone. Perhaps the man with whom she is living was unwilling, or unable financially, to marry her, but was willing to extend to her the protection of his household. Perhaps he was even a relative in the kinsman-redeemer tradition so notable in the Old Testament book of Ruth. Obviously this interpretation cannot be proved, but neither can the traditional one that labels her a harlot.

Based on this understanding of the woman's situation, I buttress my initial impression that this woman was not mocking or taunting in her earlier replies to Jesus. She was a woman hard hit by the oppression of life in first-century Palestine, and she was a realist. She knew, after five husbands and the suffering that must have accompanied those broken relationships, that endurance was all she had. She lived a life of daily hardship, grateful for food and shelter. Small wonder that she was unable to transition to Jesus' comments about her spiritual life. Life for her was very literal, dependent upon the basics of physical water, food and shelter.

Perhaps it would be helpful to consider why the woman's marital history is the aspect of her life that Jesus uses to signify his knowledge of her. Traditional exegesis has often understood it as his confrontation of her sinfulness. Suppose instead, Jesus makes this reference because it most truly represents her life situation as the victim of a system that depersonalized her. What if it is Jesus' strategy not only for revealing his supernatural knowledge, but also for expressing his compassion and concern for the suffering she has endured and the hardships she has experienced? A woman five times rejected through divorce or abandoned through death has experienced one of human life's most poignant sufferings many times. If we consider this possibility, new light is shed on this entire encounter.

I find support for this interpretation in the fact that the woman makes no effort to defend or excuse her present living arrangement. It is a fact of life; it is the best she is able to do in her "hard-knock" reality. God certainly understands. This trust in God's mercy contributes to her awakening realization of who Jesus is. His revelation that he knows her life and all that she has endured without being told, without condemning her, makes a profound impression. The probability that his remarks were expressed with compassion suggests that this man is God-like, and so she calls him a prophet. Possibly then, since he obviously possesses divine knowledge, he can answer the long-standing question about where is the proper place to worship God (4:19-20).

While many interpreters find in her question about the place of worship an attempt to deflect the conversation away from her own sinful life, again I propose an alternative view. There is evidence to suggest that she was genuinely concerned to be in proper relationship with God. After all, Jesus had expressed confidence early in his conversation with her that if she had known his identity, she would have asked him for his living water. This was a woman who lived every day in intimate contact with her need. Her trust in God and his ultimate justice and mercy may well have been the secret of her ability to endure the existence that was hers.

How much the woman understood of Jesus' description of true worship is debatable, but it apparently sounds very

God-like to her. This man had more to offer in terms of compassion, understanding, and wisdom than any prophet she had ever heard about. And so, tentatively, she brings up the matter of the Messiah (4:25).

Although the Samaritan expectation of a Messiah, a *Taheb*, was limited to the Pentateuch's promise of a prophet like Moses (Deut.18:15), they anticipated that he would have the answers for all their religious questions. She may not have understood the full import of Jesus' words, but she perceived him to be a unique being. Her testimony about expecting the Messiah could be her way of testing Jesus in comparison to that expectation. How will he relate himself to the expected Messiah? Jesus knows who she is at once; she must discover who he is, and gradually awareness is dawning.

She is beginning to recognize that Jesus is more than a man, more even than a prophet. Might he be the Messiah? After waiting hundreds of years for the prophet like Moses, fulfillment was too incredible to think. She dares not ask the question forthrightly. It is too much to consider, too overwhelming to contemplate, and yet could he be? And so she simply acknowledges her expectation to see how he will respond. In the simplest and most direct manner possible, Jesus affirms that he, the very one she is talking with so unexpectedly, is this long-awaited Messiah.

We can scarcely imagine the confusion of thoughts that must have been going through the woman's mind. The Messiah, the long expected prophet, is here! He has been conversing with her! Can it possibly be true? The literal, everyday part of her is saying this experience cannot be happening. Perhaps, this whole encounter is a dream.

Another part of her, quickened by God's Spirit, is trembling with excitement and joy and vindication. How can she know? How can she be sure? It is too overwhelming for a person to comprehend. The arrival of the disciples provides a needed interruption, for she needs time to absorb and assimilate what is happening to her. She needs help in evaluating this experience, and so she leaves her water pot and returns to the town to enlist other opinions.

The response of the townspeople to the woman's testimony is another indication that she is not an immoral, promiscuous woman. She has no trouble getting the people to hear her, to consider her question seriously. They responded by accompanying her back to the well to investigate and assess Jesus for themselves (4:29-30, 39). Had she been a loose woman with a reputation of sinfulness, I question whether she would have gotten the same response. People would more likely have jeered and mocked her, incredulous that such a person would claim to have a positive encounter with a man of God. They more likely would have laughed and ridiculed her for her testimony. Not so, this woman of John's Gospel. The people respond readily and with no resistance. The reader almost gets the opposite impression--the people are eager to believe her.

Some scholars have portrayed the woman in a positive light as a model of discipleship because she became a faithful witness and other people believed in Jesus as a result of her testimony. I have no quarrel with this understanding. I also suggest, however, that in spite of the traditional readiness to associate her with an immoral lifestyle, such a judgment is not required by the text.

This woman could have been a faithful child of God within the limits of her ability and understanding, even before her encounter with Jesus. Perhaps she was a God-fearer, not in the sense of the technical term used of Gentiles in the synagogue, but as one who acknowledged God and sought him for her daily sustenance. John states in 2:24-25 that Jesus "knew all people . . . knew what was in people." Thus it is possible to suppose that Jesus knew she was devout in her faith in spite of a life of extreme hardship and difficulty, in spite of her lowly estate within her culture. It is even possible to wonder if Jesus' need to go through Samaria was in order that he might encounter this very woman, who trusted in a gracious God regardless of what seemed a graceless life. After all, it was with just such lowly, but faithful, souls that Jesus found his best response, and the Samaritan woman did not disappoint him.

This interpretation, then, attempts to view the Samaritan woman in light of her first century social world. It is consistent with the early Church's commendation of her for her example as a faithful convert and an apostolic witness. However, this approach emphasizes the possibility of the woman's religious devotion, and her good character as well. Worshiping a God she did not fully understand (4:22), she could still have been sincere and humble in her belief. She was no less needful of Jesus' living water to restore her to proper relationship with God, but this reading delivers her from the stigma of being labeled as immoral. It enables us to see her as a believer whose faithfulness God rewarded by sending her a unique revelation. Just as promised in John's prologue, God sent her spiritual light so that she might become an enlightened child of God through her belief in Jesus Christ.

While on sabbatical at the Institute for Ecumenical and Cultural Research in Collegeville, Minnesota, during the fall semester of 2005, I attended Sunday morning worship services at the First United Methodist Church in nearby St. Cloud. Through that experience I met and found friendship with the senior pastor there who invited me to make a presentation on my racial reconciliation research to one of the church's Faith Forum meetings. This lecture is the one I shared there.

Jesus Loves the Children of the World? Christianity and Racism December 4, 2005

As Christians, we know the Bible teaches the innate dignity of all persons created in the image of God. Furthermore, by detailing the descent of all peoples from the sons of Noah (Gen. 10:1-32), the Bible declares the solidarity of all humanity through our common parentage. Differentiation and diversity were deemed "good" for humanity at creation, and God's promise to bless Abraham with a "great nation" and a "great name" provided for the continuation of blessing meant for "all peoples" (Gen. 12:2-3).

In the New Testament, Jesus Christ quite specifically calls upon the church, the people of God, to transcend national boundaries to "make disciples of all nations" (Matt. 28:19; cf. Acts 1:8). Furthermore, the essence of his teaching was love—love for God and love for neighbor. "You shall love the Lord your God with all your heart, and with all your soul, and with all your strength, and with all your mind; and your neighbor as yourself" (Luke 10:27).

Only a few decades later, the apostle Paul would comment on these two commands in his epistle to the Roman church: "Owe no one anything, except to love one another; for the one who loves another has fulfilled the law," which "is summed up in this word, "Love your neighbor as yourself" (Romans 13:8,10). Paul also speaks forthrightly of God's intention for the diverse people God created to come together in unity as one body through the person and work of Christ Jesus.

In his letter to the Ephesian Christians, Paul speaks directly to the make-up and purpose of the Church in God's eternal plan.[9] Paul acknowledges that the body of believers is composed of two ethnic groups, the Jews and the Gentiles. You remember that the Jews divided all humanity into two groups: themselves, and everybody else. Paul addresses the hostility that had historically existed between the Jews and the Gentiles—their separation and alienation from each other. But then, he delivers the deathblow to that hostility and separation and alienation by pointing out that God has overcome all these divisions through the cross of Christ.

For Christ himself has made peace between us Jews and you Gentiles by making us all one people. He has broken down the wall of hostility that used to separate us. By his death he ended[10] the whole system of Jewish law that excluded the Gentiles. His purpose was to make peace between Jews and Gentiles by creating in himself one new person from the two groups. (Eph. 2:14-16)

---

[9] Whether Paul was himself the writer of the Letter to the Ephesians, or someone writing in his style and with his theology, is irrelevant here. The letter is part of the canon of Scripture, and therefore, authoritative in its teaching for Christian believers.

[10] *Katargéw.* from the basic sense *cause to be idle* or *useless*, the term always denotes a nonphysical destruction by means of a superior force coming in to replace the force previously in effect, as, e.g. light destroys darkness.

Paul even goes on to claim that this new unity of human beings was always God's plan, but the time had to be right for God to reveal it to the weak and fallen creatures he expected to carry it out. Paul describes this plan as evidence of "the manifold wisdom of God."

His [God's] intent was that now, through the church, the manifold wisdom of God should be made known to the rulers and authorities in the heavenly realms, according to his eternal purpose which he accomplished in Christ Jesus our Lord. (Eph. 3:10-11)

The word translated as "manifold" or "in its great variety," describing God's wisdom is interesting. This Greek word, "*polypoikilos*," was often used to describe colorful embroidery on beautiful garments, and notably it is the word used in the Greek translation of the Hebrew Scriptures to describe Joseph's coat of many colors. You remember the story of that beautiful coat, which was a visible sign of his father's love for him. By analogy, the beautiful diversity that characterizes God's wisdom provides for all people, regardless of differences in skin color, culture, language, or ethnicity to live together in harmony and reciprocity.

But Paul says God has revealed this wise plan now because God intends for the people who call themselves the family of God to begin implementing this plan. So it is our job as the church to be the advance unit of what God wants his creation to be: a unified people, bringing him glory, drawn from all languages, nations, peoples, and tongues.

The end result of God's intention is pictured vividly for us in the book of Revelation. In John's vision he is permitted to see into the very throne room of God, and what he sees there is "a great multitude that no one could count, from every nation, tribe, people and language, standing before the throne and in front of the Lamb" (Rev. 7:9-10)—people who had all been "purchased for God" with the blood of the Lamb.

It seems clear to me that God's call, God's mandate, for the church, is to be a reconciling body that works to bring unity among all members of the body of Christ. Indeed, if the church is not the place where unity is pursued, where will it ever be? It is only through the power of God's Holy Spirit, transforming the hearts of sinful human beings, that we can overcome our human tendency to differentiate, to discriminate, and to alienate. In spite of racists' attempts to prove otherwise, there is no place in Christianity and the church for a theology that supports slavery or racism. The church, the body of those who follow Christ, is the one agent that has the power to achieve racial reconciliation.

Let me hasten to say that Americans have made great progress regarding race. The Civil War of the 1860s put an end to slavery, and the civil rights movement of the 1960s put an end to most racist laws and practices. And since that time there has been a growing consciousness among most Americans about the injustice of racist attitudes, talk, and behavior.

Although there is still a lot of racial hatred, few imagine that racism is acceptable today in the wider American society. But we seem to have come to the end of what can be done to rectify racism by means of legislation. What remains to be effected is the continuing change in the hearts of people, and that has to happen one person at a time. The laws of our nation support racial equality, and for many Americans it is supported by Christian faith, but it is still not inevitable.

Based on the biblical texts I have mentioned, in addition to many I didn't reference, it seems clear to me that racial reconciliation—not racial segregation—is the attitude consistent with the Christian understanding of God and human history. The eternal intention of God is that all peoples should live together in peace and harmony, a peace and harmony pictured in the culminating book of the New Testament. It describes a scene of praising the Lamb by all those whom Jesus purchased with his blood for God, "members of every tribe and language and people and nation." (Rev. 5:9).

How then, do we as the redeemed people of God, who have been reconciled with God by the saving work of Jesus Christ, work to be reconciled with our brothers and sisters in God's family who are different from us in some way? I think we have to begin by acknowledging that there are no easy answers. Racial reconciliation is hard work. It requires us to be more like Jesus and less like the rest of our society. But most of us are creatures of conformity, and it is difficult for us to be counter-cultural, to swim against the current. And yet, isn't that what Jesus' radical call to discipleship is all about--to shun the broad and popular path and to follow him on the narrow and difficult way? That basic issue is one each of us must struggle with and work out between our own souls and God, but making the assumption that we all WANT to live as God would have us to live, let's look at some particulars.

First of all, we have to acknowledge our own complicity in the structures of racism. Joseph Barndt, a pastor in the Bronx in New York City, argues that "racism in the United States is not only an issue between Blacks and whites, it is an issue of power, domination, and control that defines white America's relationship with Native Americans, Hispanics, and Asian Americans."[11]

The reality is that "whites have benefited from the structure of racism whether they have ever committed a racist act,

---

[11] Joseph Barndt. *Dismantling Racism* (Minneapolis: Augsburg, 1991), viii.

uttered a racist word, or uttered a racist thought. Just as surely as African Americans and other people of color suffer in a white society because they are African Americans, Native Americans, Hispanics, or Asians, whites benefit because they are white."[12]

So I think one of the most important steps in overcoming racism is to recognize "our own unknowing complicity in the institutional aspects of racism and summoning up the will to challenge the status quo in our immediate surroundings."[13] To a large extent, racism is a white problem because to be maximally effective, change has to take place within the white community.

In order to begin taking responsibility for changing the racism that continues to plague the church and the world, Curtiss Paul DeYoung, Professor of Reconciliation Studies at Bethel University in St. Paul, Minnesota, suggests the following steps:

1. Recognize that reconciliation is a process.

2. Discover and recognize the truth of the racism that exists.

Karen McKinney, an experiential educator, uses an exercise called "The Race" to help individuals identify how the effects of injustice impact their lives. Participants line up side by side, but then they must answer a series of questions in the "qualifying" round to determine their placement at the starting line. She asks questions about the number of books in their homes, how many see their parents reading books, how many see authority figures that look like them, how many parents work in white-collar jobs, etc. As you can imagine, there is great disparity between most of the

---

[12] Ibid., ix.
[13] Ronice Branding. *Fulfilling the Dream: Confronting the Challenge of Racism* (St. Louis: Chalice Press, 1998) 3.

minority children and the white children. These disparities are reflected in limitations that cause the minority children to enter the "race" of life not at the starting line with the white children, but far behind them. They begin the race already at a place of disadvantage. Those in back try hard to win but can't overcome the odds; those far behind the starting line often just give up. This exercise is a vivid illustration of the distinctions in society that result from injustice and how they affect our lives and fuel the continuation of division between whites and minorities.

3. Seek forgiveness. Forgiveness opens the door to reconciliation and relationship. Without it, we cannot move forward toward peace and equality.

4. Where possible, we need to repair the wrong done. Repairing the wrong that was committed is a way to restore trust and should help to reconstruct the equality of social and economic relationships, as well as create a just balance of power within society and the church.

Regardless of the setting, "acts of justice need to include both reparation of physical damage and reparation of systemic damage. Declaring that we all are equal without repairing the wrongs of the past is cheap reconciliation."[14]

5. Give birth to communities of the reconciled, recognizing that it will require us to live in the tension of agreeing to disagree without disrespecting one another and without withdrawing when the going gets tough.[15]

Speaking specifically for churches and Christians, what might a focus on the ministry of reconciliation look like? It is important to realize that "every church in America today

---

[14] Curtiss Paul DeYoung. *Reconciliation: Our Greatest Challenge—Our Only Hope* (Valley Forge: Judson Press, 1997), 106.
[15] These ideas are derived from DeYoung, 87-97.

is communicating some message about the relevance of salvation in Jesus Christ to the racial situation in our country and about God's ability to heal the divisions separating humanity. . ... More specifically, each Christian communicates a great deal about the relevance of salvation in Jesus Christ to racial reconciliation and whether God has endowed his children with any special gift that can heal the racial divisions separating people."[16]

Norman A. Peart, a sociologist and founding pastor of a multiracial church in Cary, North Carolina, has assessed five types of churches or models of reconciliation according to what he calls the reconciliation continuum. They range from segregationist churches at one extreme, which are totally exclusive, and fully integrated multicultural churches at the other, which are totally inclusive. In between are churches involved in some way in moving toward reconciliation.

For example, the differentiation model allows for the possibility of sharing spaces—worship and educational buildings—but there is no interaction between the two groups of Christians. Each conducts its own familiar style of worship and church activities. The assimilation model welcomes incoming members of different racial or ethnic groups, but makes no adjustments to accommodate the uniqueness of these members. They are expected to become like the majority or dominant group and no provision is made to allow their cultural distinctions to influence what is already being done.

In what Peart calls the intentional but irrational model, the church intentionally works to bring members of another group in and also works to have their culture and uniqueness represented throughout the ministry. This is a

---

[16] Norman Anthony Peart. *Separate No More: Understanding and Developing Racial Reconciliation in Your Church* (Grand Rapids: Baker Books, 2000), 127, 129.

genuine effort, but its weakness is its failure to acknowledge the racial and ethnic differences. It creates an artificial environment that exists only when and where the church's members gather; outside the church there is no unity. The church doesn't transform the prejudices and thoughts of its members by addressing them openly, but suppresses them for the sake of unity. This church's view of unity in Christ means that no one expresses discontent or displeasure much less raises racial issues or challenges racial views lest they be considered contentious.

Peart's most desirable model is what he terms "inHIMtegration," by which he means a church that "makes intentional choices to mix, accept, represent, and manifest racial and ethnic differences, but at the same time magnifies to a greater extent the oneness of believers in Christ." This model seeks to bring to fruition the new humanity created in Christ, which Paul describes in Ephesians 2:13-16. This model "begins with the premise that believers are already one in Christ and must not live the divisiveness that surrounds them. [They] must challenge the erroneous beliefs and actions they and their fellow believers have come to accept as reality. As the black historian John Hope Franklin puts it, "You change hearts by changing heads."[17]

This model's strength is that it recognizes that racism is interwoven into our society, yet it works to magnify the spiritual reality of the unity that exists for believers in Christ. It also has the advantage of allowing individuals to express pride in their culture and heritage as an aspect of their identity in Christ.[18]

Our nation and our people have come a long way since 1619 when black people and white people first came to this country under equal conditions. That long journey has had

---

[17] Ibid, 130-140.
[18] Ibid, 141.

its low points and its high points. In terms of legal equality, perhaps we are nearing the apex of our ability to legislate fair and equal treatment for all, but in terms of our societal and individual character, we are still on the upward journey.

Listen to the words of Jim Lo, an Asian American college professor and former missionary to South Africa and Cambodia:

In obedience to God, the Church in North America must choose acceptance of, and cultural sensitivity to, those from different ethnic backgrounds. If that is to happen, it must begin with individual Christians—like you—[and me]—who are willing to move out of their comfort zones and intentionally create relationships with people of other cultures.[19]

My hope is that after considering these thoughts you will have reached two conclusions: First, racial reconciliation is not an option for Christians; it is part of our calling in the family of God. Second, racial reconciliation is not easy; in fact, it is hard. And it will not happen of its own accord. If we want to live now in the community of faith that God intends for us for all eternity, we must pursue racial reconciliation intentionally. We will make mistakes; we will need to be forgiven; and we will need to persevere.

---

[19] *Intentional Diversity: Creating Cross-Cultural Ministry Relationships in Your Church* (Indianapolis: Wesleyan Publishing House, 2002), 13.

www.ingramcontent.com/pod-product-compliance
Lightning Source LLC
Chambersburg PA
CBHW052142110526
44591CB00012B/1825